# FROM A SPARK COMES A FLAME

## A Spin Off Novella from The Horses Know Trilogy

LYNN MANN

Coxstone Press

ISBN 978-1-7393276-0-6
Published by Coxstone Press 2023

*In honour of Eden*

ONE

## Fitt

I perch awkwardly at Katonia and Jack's kitchen table in the predawn darkness. My chair is too small for me and I worry that its legs won't take my full weight, so I partly sit and partly hover. It would be easier to sit on the ground as I'm accustomed to doing, but I'll be spending a lot of time in the homes of humans in the months and years to come, so I'm determined to find a way to negotiate their living arrangements and customs.

To that end, my fingers curl around the mug of steaming tea I've made for myself. I have to find a way to drink it from the vessels in which it is bound to be offered, but as yet I haven't found a way to do it without spilling the hot liquid down my chin. When we Kindred drink, we usually pour fluid into our mouths from cupped hands or leaves. Trying to position a small, thick brimmed mug between my fangs so that I can drink as humans do is nowhere near as straightforward.

My parents, and the other Kindred who came with us to Rockwood, are very happy with the drinking bowls – shallow and with thin brims that taper outward – that Justin has made for them. I envy them the ease with which they are integrating into the village; they don't even attempt to sit on chairs and at tables that weren't built for their weight and size, they welcome humans to sit alongside them on the thick rugs that cover the grey flagstones of the village's cottages during wintertime.

But this is their home now. It isn't mine; I will be leaving for other villages very soon, where I will need to be able to accept whatever hospitality is offered to me in order to be accepted by those I want to help – those who will already be afraid of me without me making my differences even more obvious.

I look down at my body for what must be the hundredth time since arriving in Rockwood with Flame five days ago. Whereas I used to feel the shame and revulsion of my ancestors whenever I had cause to regard any part of myself, now I feel an acceptance of my physical appearance that has a ring of the obvious about it, as if it were always there waiting to be uncovered under the layers of negativity instilled into my bloodline by the humans of The Old.

I accept that, while my face verifies my human heritage in shape and features, it is covered with fine brown hair that no human female face would ever yield. I accept that the pupils of my eyes, and the fangs that prevent me from smiling as fully as the humans I have come to hold dear, are the result of my feline heritage. I accept that my avian DNA is responsible for the talons that, while useful, can be deadly. And I accept the crustacean genes that make my skin thick and tough, and that my flat nose, powerfully muscled body and wiry hair are the result of the ape genes that contribute to who I am.

But even though I accept all of those things, it doesn't mean I find it easy when the humans of Rockwood rest their eyes upon me. While I am Aware that they feel no ill will towards me, their curiosity at my appearance and how I am similar to them yet so very dissimilar; their wonder as they peruse their Awareness of how the scientists of The Old managed to create my ancestors, the Enforcers of their cities; their pondering of my body's capabilities and the uses to which I put it before Amarilla and Infinity befriended me, all result in everything for which I forgave humans of both The Old and The New stirring uncomfortably within me.

Those who have achieved sufficient Awareness sense my discomfort, and blood rushes to their faces, causing them to turn the deep pink of which mine will never be capable. Their heart rates increase as they instinctively fear my reaction, and while the bravest of them manage to slow and deepen their breathing before rushing to my side and apologising for their intrusion, the less courageous lose the fight to control themselves and flee from my vicinity as quickly as they can.

I can cope with it, of course I can. Whenever I feel myself being knocked off centre, I only have to shift my focus to Flame and all she is in order to remember that no harm has been done to me, for the potential to do so does not exist – the energy of forgiveness, to which my Bond-Partner introduced me, is powerful and absolute. Then, the determination I share with my beautiful Bond-Partner will flare inside me and I'll find myself itching to leave Rockwood and travel far and wide to the villages of The New so that I can bring their inhabitants to Awareness.

But the time for that isn't now. Now, if I am to achieve my purpose in this life, I have to work harder at being able to fit in. I lift the mug of tea – which I am relieved to find smells exactly as it's supposed to since I have removed the leaves and added the honey most humans prefer – level with my mouth and contemplate my next attempt to drink from it.

'How about drinking it the way you prefer?' Am shuffles into the kitchen wrapped in a blanket, her hair knotted and sticking out to the side on which she's been lying, her eyes still full of sleep. She collides with a chair and winces. 'I know you can see in the dark, Fitt, but do you mind if I light a lamp for me? The clouds must still be heavy with snow for them to be blocking out the light of the moon so completely.'

'Let me.' I smile with satisfaction as I manage to grasp one of the tiny matches my friends use, strike it against its box without snapping it, and hold it inside the bulb of the lamp until light flares, casting shadows on the kitchen walls.

'You can always use the long tapers we use to light the fire,' Am says, pulling a chair away from the table with her foot and almost collapsing atop it as she trips over the bottom of her blanket.

'I can use these,' I reply.

'And you know there's a pile of bowls in the cupboard for you to drink from, as well as a good stock of tea leaves,' Am adds, 'so feel free to add more to your tea and leave them in so it gets as strong as I know you prefer it.' She stares at me, her blue eyes serious.

'Thanks, but I want to drink it like this.'

She sighs. 'No you don't, and actually, it's important that you don't.' She looks up above me for emphasis rather than necessity, for I feel it too; the energy of possibility, inevitability, even, that began to swirl around me whilst we were on our way here from Shady Mountain.

But I refuse to be distracted from the task that I have arisen especially early to attempt by myself without the exact kind of interference that Amarilla is intent on providing.

'There's being determined and there's being stubborn,' my friend tells me as she rubs her eyes, 'and right now, you're being stubborn. We all know what you're trying to do and why, but as everyone who loves you has already told you, and as you know for yourself deep down, it isn't the way to go.' She leans forward and weaves her face around until I can't stop my eyes straying from the mug I am once again holding up to my mouth, to look at her.

I sigh and slam the mug down. It smashes and tea creeps across the table. I leap to my feet, causing my chair to fly backward with a crash, and knocking into the table so that the fluid spreads more quickly. It's only as I hurry back from the sink with a cloth that I notice the back of the chair has separated from its seat.

I spread the cloth over the spilt tea, trying to avoid my friend's eyes even though I can't for I feel them boring into me every bit as much as I feel the affection that accompanies their stare.

Amarilla's small, delicate, perfect human hand with its perfectly formed fingers and nails comes to rest upon my huge, hairy, taloned one.

*We've always been completely honest with one another, you and I.* Her thought is warm and carries memories of when we first met – when I was struggling to hunt on my Findself and she was intent on helping me.

Her fingers close around my hand, which she lifts from the wet cloth and encloses within both of hers – or tries to for it is an impossibility. She allows the blanket to fall from her shoulders as she gets to her feet and pulls on my hand. I can't help but follow her; if I resist her movement then my talons will slice through her hands.

She leads me to the side of the table and sits down cross-legged on the thick, blue rug that prevents the cold of winter from escaping the flagstones below. It is only when I sit down opposite her that she releases my hand. Her eyes glitter in the lamplight.

*You're afraid, Fitt, I know that. You're determined to succeed and you're frightened you won't because of how the villagers you'll meet will react to you.* She continues out loud, 'I get it, the light knows I do, but I don't think being able to sit on a chair that's too small for you, drinking tea from a mug is what will make the difference.' She holds her hands up in front of her. 'I'm sorry. I also get that you need to work this through for yourself, so you can consider me formally getting off your case. Flame is all you need.'

At the mention of my Bond-Partner, everything around me fades away – Amarilla, the loudly ticking grandfather clock whose shadow flickers against the wall behind her, the broken chair beside me, the smell of honey-sweetened tea.

Flame is standing with Infinity, her ears pricked as she listens intently to a vixen screaming for potential suitors just beyond the paddock fence. The two horses extend their senses to where a dog fox moves stealthily through the snow some distance away, then to an even wider area. When they decide in the same breath that there is nothing of which to be alarmed, they return their attention to the hay racks in Candour's field shelter. Since the solid structure of grey stone was designed for a single horse, it's a bit of a squeeze for the two of them, but Infinity's petite stature makes it just about possible for them to share it.

My Bond-Partner is content, as she always is now that she's free of everything that used to weigh on her body and soul. Her warmth, for which Amarilla named her, becomes all of me along with our determination to forge ahead on the mission that we agreed, so long ago in the place that is everywhere and nowhere, to undertake. I forget the differences between me and those I would help, and feel only jubilation that I will be able to help them and as a consequence, my own kind.

My own kind. The words seem to hang in the air, pulling me away from Flame's influence and back to the broken chair and the tea that has now begun to drip slowly from the table. My own kind are depending on me to help the humans of The New to Awareness so that they will know we Kindred for who we really are; so that they will be Aware we mean them no harm, that we would live alongside them and contribute to their wellbeing and evolution even as we hope they will assist us with ours. It has to be me who performs the task. I alone am both Kindred and Horse-Bonded, my heritage giving me the ability to connect with and bring Awareness to humans, my horse affording me credibility and the ability to travel at speed so that I can spread Awareness far and wide.

It has to be me. Me, who would never have survived my Findself without help. Me, who was raised to Kindred Elder before having a chance to gain the experience to perform the role with any level of confidence. Me, who is newly bonded and on top of that, has a different bond with Flame than those shared by all of the other Horse-Bonded with their horses; while I love the fact that we are more of one another than any other bonded pair except perhaps for Amarilla and Infinity, and as such have always responded to one another without need for conscious thought, I sometimes envy my bonded friends for the mindspeak conversations they have with their horses.

When I'm succumbing to the fear that I can't blame upon my heritage, my upbringing, my current situation or anything else, it would be good to have Flame counsel me in the same way my parents do, in the same way my friends do, in a way that would make me the same as all of the Horse-Bonded when all I can seem to focus upon is how I am different.

A burst of warmth from Flame incinerates my worries and insecurities all over again.

I meet Amarilla's gaze. 'Flame may be all I need but that doesn't mean you're wrong. No more chairs and mugs.'

She gets to her knees, shuffles across the rug and hugs me. 'No more chairs and mugs.'

I strap my bow and arrows to my back. The second they are in place, Katonia busies herself by sliding her fingers along the length of the straps to ensure they aren't twisted. Then she pulls at them sharply.

'They're secure, you're good to go,' she tells me as if I didn't already know. She rubs her hands up and down my arms and adds, 'Are you sure you'll be warm enough? I mean, I know you will be, you've survived this long without clothes in winter, it's just that, well it's just that...'

'You want to look after her the way you do the rest of us,' Jack says gently, putting an arm around his wife's shoulders and stepping backward so that he draws her away from me. He tightens his hold around her and she hugs him back. 'Thanks for doing what you're about to for us all, Fitt,' he says to me. 'We'll visit your parents often while you're gone, and if there's anything they need for their new home, we'll make sure they have it.'

I smile gratefully. 'Thank you, and thanks for having me here these past few weeks.'

'Are you absolutely sure you won't stay until spring?' Katonia says. 'I know you don't feel the cold like we do but you're also used to staying within the shelter of the trees, and you'll be travelling across country where the wind will catch you.'

'I'm sure.'

Katonia looks up at me, her eyes so like those of her sister's in shape and colour but softer, less intense. I sense her Awareness touching mine and she remembers that just as she has her role to play in these times of change, I have mine. The softness of her voice matches that of her gaze as she says, 'We love you, Fitt, you and Flame, and everyone you're going to meet will too.' She straightens her back. 'But if you need a break from them, or from travelling, at any time, you come straight back here. And if you need any help, with anything at all, you let me know. Do you understand?'

Amarilla chuckles from behind me. 'Wow. I never thought I'd say this, Kat, but you just reminded me of Mum.'

'I'm glad you said it,' Justin says, 'I was wondering if it was just me.' Their observation lifts the mood and I can't help smiling as Jack leaps to his wife's defence.

I nod to Katonia, who is also smiling as she continues to watch me, her keen Awareness missing nothing. *I understand. Thank you, Katonia, for everything.*

'Ready for the off?' Marvel's voice proceeds him and Rowena as they stamp as much snow from their boots as they can outside the door, then step into the kitchen.

'Sorry about this, Kat,' Rowena says, looking down at their feet where the remaining snow is rapidly melting into a puddle. 'The snow's deep enough to be clean, so do you mind if we keep our boots on? If we take them off, they're going to be horrid to put back on.'

Katonia waves a dismissive hand at their wet boots. 'Yes of course. We have spare boots here you can change into though if you like, and I can dry yours out and drop them back to you at Jasmine and Jodral's when they're wearable again?'

Rowena looks between Amarilla and Katonia and shakes her head in amazement. 'I've said it before and I'll say it again, Am.'

'How did you two spring from the same womb?' the rest of us chorus.

Rowena pretends she hasn't heard us. 'How DID you two

spring from the same womb? It's like a riddle set by nature to confuse the rest of us.'

Marvel grins as he looks around at us all. 'Riddle of nature, you say, Ro. I, for one, find it interesting that you've had the time to notice they exist when there are so many people incapable of getting through each day without your input.'

I grin along with everyone else as we all sense another of Marvel and Rowena's pretend arguments brewing. I'm going to miss them all so much.

It's tempting, all of a sudden, to accept Katonia's invitation to stay here for a few months, to allow myself the comfort of being with those I love for a little bit longer. But then a familiar warmth increases in my mind. Flame. I'll be with her, and with Sonja and Bright, Aleks and Nexus. Aleks is determined to explore everything of which he is now capable, and as soon as he volunteered to come with me, Sonja's mind was set on doing the same.

My eyes meet Amarilla's as everyone else takes a side in the ongoing teasing between Marvel and Rowena. My friend is weary despite a few weeks' rest. She has achieved much in the past few years, and she needs time to catch up with herself, to settle into the choices she has made and the person she has become. Both of us smile as we sense again the swirl of energy that was once attached to her but now accompanies me. If she is to truly rest, I need to remove myself, and the vortex of change that I have become, from Rockwood. The realisation combines with Flame's reminder of what we are about, and galvanises me into action.

Amarilla watches me knowingly as I head for the door. When I reach it, I turn and say as loudly as my raspy voice will allow, 'Jack and Katonia, thanks again. Rowena and Marvel, have a good journey back to The Gathering. Amarilla and Justin, don't work too hard on the Histories, there'll always be more to write and always enough time to write it. As I told my parents last night, I'd prefer it if we could save our hugs until we meet again.' Like my parents, they all know I won't be able to leave unless we do. I pause for a short breath before adding, 'Fare you well, my friends.'

Their thoughts combine into a single one that is rapidly echoed by my parents, Vickery, Holly and the rest of the Kindred who came with me to Rockwood... and then by everyone else currently hunkering down in the village's cottages, out of the wind and snow.

*Take our love with you, Fitt.*

I do. It carries me through the driving snow to where Flame is waiting for me by the paddock gate, her brown eyes soft and warm as she blinks away the snowflakes that land upon her orange eyelashes. She whickers to me and shakes her body from head to tail, dislodging the snow that formed a second coat over her own woolly one. Infinity waits at her side but moves away obligingly so that I can approach my horse, onto whose back I leap from a standstill.

'About time too, we're freezing,' Aleks bellows above the wind from the other side of the fence. I can only just make out Nexus beneath him, her grey coat making her almost invisible in the blizzard even as her large, dark eyes peer at me between the snowflakes.

'I'll get the gate,' Sonja hollers and Bright sidles closer to the fence, his dark fur almost completely obscured by the white layer of snow that swathes him and his Bond-Partner.

'I've got it,' Amarilla yells, hauling the gate through the deepening snow. When there is a wide enough opening for Flame to carry me through, she sweeps the snow from Infinity's back, climbs the fence and mounts her horse while telling me, 'I'm just here to accompany Fin to my parents' paddock so she can be with Gas, and Candour can come home.'

We both know that all three horses could have waited.

Sonja glances between my friend and me, then says to Aleks, 'Come on then, we'll lead the way, shall we?'

Bright and Nexus turn and head for the paddock of Nixonhouse. Flame and Infinity follow them, walking side by side as they have so many times before.

Amarilla and I don't speak, we just enjoy the simple companionship we've always cherished while our horses do the same, until we reach the paddock that Candour has been sharing with the Nixons' donkeys. From there, Aleks, Sonja and I continue onward, leaving Amarilla to dismount from Infinity at the paddock gate.

A squeal tells my ears that Candour has left the field shelter in favour of greeting Infinity, as surely as her feigned outrage informs my Awareness of the event. A thudding of hooves through snow accompanies Candour's instigation of a game in which Infinity is more than happy to partake. Their enjoyment is infectious and Flame picks up her pace beneath me so that she moves level with Nexus and Bright. All three horses draw themselves up taller than their normal heights as Candour and Infinity blast past and then around in front of us, Candour bucking as Infinity spins on the spot and rears before the two of them plough through the snow back the way we have all come.

None of our three horses even consider following them, but rather take their energy and encouragement and leap forward as one into a jubilant, powerful, snow-defeating canter. Six hearts beat with a single purpose as we leave Rockwood behind.

# TWO

## Sonja

*I* am relieved when the horses slow to a walk; they are on the verge of sweating, and I don't want sweat freezing on them and cooling them dangerously.

'We must be flaming well insane to be travelling in this when we don't have to,' Aleks yells, his eyes shining and cheeks rosy above the relaxed smile that belies his words.

I can't help smiling with him, just as I haven't been able to stop smiling since Fitt accepted our offer to travel with her. 'It's exciting, isn't it? Thanks for having us along with you, Fitt, I know you'll miss Am and Fin but hopefully Aleks and I can be half decent substitutes.'

Fitt grimaces momentarily at my mention of the two to whom she feels closest in the world besides Flame and her parents. If she were apart from Flame it would have been for longer than a moment, but since she's astride and in balance with her mare, the slight hardening of Fitt's mouth, the catch of her breath, the stiffening of her shoulders all fade as quickly as they arose.

'Thank you for your company,' she says, the rasp in her voice more discernible due to the effort of raising it above the bitterly cold wind. The affection and gratitude that accompany her words negate the necessity for her to say anything else.

Aleks glances across at me and raises his eyebrows at also having perceived the slight discomfort that preceded her thanks. I shrug briefly in return, acknowledging the courage we both know it has taken for Fitt to leave Rockwood and travel to the villages with only Aleks and me along with her to try to ease the fears of those who will find her help difficult to accept.

I watch our friend out of the corner of my eye as our horses plough through the snow even as more continues to fall and deepen it further. Fitt is truly remarkable. Her powerfully muscled, hairy body, with its long arms and relatively short legs, shouldn't look so natural upon the back of such an elegant horse, but it does. She sits easily, not appearing to do anything other than absorb her horse's movement, yet Flame, as always, moves with more power and strength than when Fitt isn't astride her. The two of them go beyond the oneness that is obvious when any of we Horse-Bonded ride our horses; they amplify one another so that rather than just merging into a single being, they burn with everything they are, fuelling one another to ever greater potential.

I'm hoping – we're all hoping – that it will be enough to sustain Fitt when she isn't physically with her horse. Like all of us, she can be with Flame in her mind whenever she wants to, and in fact has always done so to a greater extent than most of us due to having been born Aware. But she can also, like all of us, be knocked from her centre.

Aleks interrupts my thoughts. 'It's only been a week since…' The rest of his words are lost in the wind. He pulls his scarf up around his face so that only his eyes are showing, and tries again.

His thought is full of enthusiasm. *It's only been a week since the Heralds left Rockwood to spread word of our impending visit to the villages. I hope that means that the first few at least will have shelter ready and waiting for our horses, and nice hot meals and warm beds waiting for us.*

I sense Fitt's amusement matching mine; Aleks may have let go of his dependency on physical comfort but that doesn't mean he doesn't still appreciate it. Also typical of Aleks is the fact that his thoughts continue in a steady stream without need or opportunity for any response from the two of us.

*Amarilla said Bigwood's normally half a day's ride away but at the rate we're going, it'll be almost evening by the time we get there. We can eat as we ride but there'll be slim pickings for the horses. Mind you, we'll be riding through the big wood that the village is named after, won't we? I'm sure that's what Katonia said, so hopefully the horses will be able to browse a little on the way through. I still find it strange to travel through woodland without needing to be alert for Kindred staring at us and hunting the horses. You'd think I'd have got used to it by now, wouldn't you, especially as one of us is a Kindred? I mean...*

I'm distracted by the warmth that blazes with even more intensity from Fitt at the mention of her being one of us. As with her momentary discomfort before, it disappears almost as soon as it arrived, absorbed by the inferno of love, courage and determination that is her horse.

*...and as for Levitsson, he just gets funnier and funnier. If only he were Horse-Bonded, he'd have been able to come with us. I mean, goodness knows, he could do with a break from Foxstep breathing down his neck and telling him to watch what he says when in fact, his honesty is a breath of fresh air. He's helping so many people past their blocks to greater Awareness with his*

*directness and levity – hey, I wonder if it runs in his family, I mean, their names all start with "Levits". Get it? Levits and levity? But then you're all named down your female lines after members of the original Kindred from The Old, aren't you, Fitt? Still though, Levitsson's original ancestor could have chosen that particular Kindred to name herself after because she had an affinity with the idea of possessing levity, couldn't she? I wish my Awareness stretched to the past and future the way Am's does, but I still don't get the whole "time is non-linear" thing. I don't think I ever will but that's fine because...*

Fitt looks sidelong at me, her mouth curling up slightly at its edges in as much of a smile as her fangs allow. I smile back, Aware how fond she is of the man I am growing to love. Where others can find him irritating, Fitt enjoys his company and admires him for the courage he has had to employ so often during his life in order to function in a world where his fellow humans haven't always understood him. She played a significant role in helping him past his fears to the happy person he is today, something neither Aleks nor I will either forget. Helping and supporting her on her mission is the least we can do in return, and we have both resolved to do whatever we can, whatever it takes, for her to succeed.

We all dip our heads as the wind whips snow into our faces with even greater force, strong enough even to disrupt Aleks's mental discourse. Bright, beneath me, feels no discontent despite the discomfort of snow assaulting his eyeballs faster than he can blink it away, and the effort of forging a path through the ever deepening snow. As far as he is concerned, the weather isn't bad; he makes no judgement of it at all and as a result has no need for it to be easier. Not for the first time, I wish I could see things as he does.

*That is entirely your choice,* he reminds me, also not for the first time. *When you relinquish your need to be warm then the cold will have no sway over you. When you do not view being dry as more desirable than being wet then you will be free of the need to observe and assess the weather so closely.*

*But it's been my job to observe and manipulate the weather for such a long time, I can't help being more sensitive to it than most,* I reply. *I've loved being a Weather-Singer, I've loved bringing better weather to areas that have needed it, and I've spent so long ensuring that I'm constantly attuned to it that I struggle to dismiss it as an irrelevance.*

*The choice to struggle is also yours.*

I sigh. *I know. Honestly, Bright, I wonder how you put up with me.*

*I am unaffected by your decision to feel a certain way in the same way that I am unaffected by the weather.*

*By not judging it as good or bad. I get it, I'll try to do better.*

*You will learn much by observing He Who Is Nexus and She Who Is Flame more closely in that regard.*

I look across at Aleks in surprise. Fitt, riding between us, is as emotionally unaffected by the weather as are the horses, but I am Aware that Aleks's discomfort is almost on a level with mine.

*It's easier for Fitt,* I tell Bright, *she doesn't feel the cold nearly as much as we do. What do you mean about Aleks though?*

*She Who Is Flame has become well practised at altering her perception of events. She walks to her full height as a consequence. He Who Is Nexus followed her example and released himself from the hold of his past.*

*Fitt forgave us humans, and Aleks forgave himself. Being able to tolerate the weather is about forgiveness? Ah, I see, it's the same. It's about not judging anything as bad. So I need to forgive the weather for it to lose its influence on my state of mind?*

*It will serve all three of you to be able to forgive anything that you have afforded the ability to affect you. He Who Is Nexus does it constantly in order to tolerate the judgements made of his differences by those who know no better. She Who Is Flame is but a spark of whom she will be when she can forgive those who would torment her in this lifetime as easily as she forgave those who tormented her ancestors. Her Bond-Partner will help her but she will need the examples of He Who Is Nexus and She Who Is Bright to remind her of the way forward when she is most challenged. You have made the weather important to you. See it as it really is and you will be as strong as He Who Is Nexus in the support you can provide.*

I glance across at Aleks again, only just able to make him out in the blizzard. Bright is right, as always; Aleks has always been the subject of interest, teasing and irritation due to his ways, and he used to tolerate it largely because he was unaware of it. Since becoming Aware, however, he always knows when he is being regarded with curiosity or irritation and yet is always cheerful and friendly to everyone, regardless of their feelings towards him. I hadn't considered how or why that is until now, I've just enjoyed his company, but my heart swells with an even greater level of admiration for him now that I realise how much I have to learn from him – how adept he is at employing the concept Fitt imparted to us last summer.

*Aleks, Bright has just advised that if we give up our judgement of the weather, we'll take away its ability to make us feel miserable.*

Fitt nods in agreement and Aleks is only a few heartbeats behind. *AMAZING!* His thought is so full of joy, my lips crack as I smile. *Why did I not realise that? It's so much easier than forgiving myself for being such an arse when I incarnated in The Old. Thanks, Bright. Come on, Sonn, you're still miserable. Let go of hating the cold and you'll shiver happily instead of letting it get to you.*

*Everything in me wants to draw up warm air from the south to make it warmer, even though I know it's not appropriate to try to change seasonal weather to such a degree. How do I push all of my learning, my instincts, my experience and ability aside?* I ask Aleks, then become Aware of the answer to my question from both him and Fitt as they remember forgiving an energy far more malevolent than the blizzard that is bothering me. They did it by trusting their horses and their friends.

*You can do it, Sonn,* Aleks confirms, *and you must be ready to or Bright wouldn't have brought it up.*

*Trust him in this as much as you have trusted him in everything else,* Fitt advises.

I sense the weight of their experience behind me, pushing me forward to the decision I don't want to make in case it changes how I see myself – in case it changes who I am. I am Sonja Nieversen, Bond-Partner to Bright and one of the strongest Weather-Singers recorded in the Histories. If I decide to see the weather as an irrelevance, who will I be? Will my ability to sing up a torrent in order to quench a forest fire be affected? Will I be able to use the force of my will to sing up a wind strong enough to shift a troublesome rainstorm if I don't see it as a problem? Amarilla helped me to release my need to be important, but releasing another part of myself, one that has allowed me to contribute to my community – do I really want to release that?

*Re-centre yourself and you will know,* Bright advises me.

The second that my Awareness of my connection to him and all else balances my personality's concerns, my fears dissipate. I am She Who Is Bright. I blast light out around myself in confirmation… and feel comfortable in my cold, shivering skin.

*Self-identity is important to humans,* Bright informs me. *It affords a level of confidence and strength that your fellow humans will recognise. Your decision to settle into yours is well timed. You convinced yourself that She Who Is Flame travels with companions who are less than she deserves. He Who Is Nexus was always the best choice to accompany her. You have now joined him in suitability.*

# THREE

## Aleks

*J*ust because the wind and snow haven't affected my sense of wellbeing since following Bright's counsel, it doesn't mean I'm not relieved to reach the cover of the trees for which the village of Bigwood was named. The wind now howls far above us and the snow flutters gently between the evergreen branches as the trees spare us the viciousness of winter while simultaneously treating us to its beauty.

Snow is heaped precisely but precariously on boughs and twigs, every now and then thudding to the ground as a result of the flake that has been sufficient to tip its balance. The forest floor is a thick blanket of white, punctuated only by the odd bramble or tree stump. The animals are mostly quiet but the voices of those who do call seem purer and louder through the heavy silence. The air is sharp and clean, as if the snow and trees have acted together to strip it bare.

I turn around to Fitt and Sonja, whose horses are picking their way between the trees behind Nexus, and say, 'It's good to finally be able to hear myself think.'

Fitt makes the raspy sound that used to terrify me before I learnt that it's her version of a laugh. 'We heard you loud and clear, my friend.' I sense her affection for me as she continues, 'Your enthusiasm is infectious and your ability to take Bright's counsel inspiring.'

'I couldn't agree more,' Sonja says, pulling her scarf down from her face to reveal rosy cheeks and a few wisps of auburn hair that have escaped her thick, woollen hat. 'Thanks, Aleks, and you, Fitt, for adding your support to Bright's, I should have just followed his advice straight away.'

I spit out the snow that has just flicked into my mouth from a low growing twig I didn't see until the last moment, and say, 'What you should stop doing is being so hard on yourself.'

'Aleks is right, you're...' Fitt splutters as the disturbance I created in the tree that I have now passed, results in a load of snow landing on her from higher up.

I grin in delight. Fitt shakes her head to dislodge the snow atop it but a small pile remains in an almost perfect pyramid. I start to laugh. I stop when a snowball hits me full in the face, then begin again when I sense Sonja's mirth. Flaming lanterns, she's a good shot.

That does it. The snowballs fly as quickly as we can scrape snow from our horses' backs and nearby branches to form them. It is only when I notice the trees beginning to thin out and the wind catching me once more, that I turn to face forward and realise that the horses have stoically carried us through the forest to the village that now lies just ahead.

I lean forward and stroke Nexus's neck. *Sorry about that.*

*The hilarity that resulted from your game was necessary. I have no complaint.*

I am Aware that neither Flame nor Bright are perturbed either. Sonja, on the other hand, is pretending to be mightily so. Riding at the back of our short procession through the trees, she alone had no protection from the snowballs aimed at her; I could avoid both Fitt's and her snowballs by turning to face the front for a moment or two, and Fitt could avoid Sonja's as easily, if not mine. As Sonja hastily attempts to brush clumps of snow off her hat, cloak and legs, she huffs and puffs, her protestations getting louder with each stroke.

'Are you going to blow the house down?' I call back to her over the wind which is now alone in its ferocity since the snow has finally stopped falling. 'The moral of this particular story is, don't start a snowball fight when you're the one with the least cover. Your releasing your attachment to being warm and dry couldn't have come at a better time, could it?' She laughs the tinkling laugh that I find so endearing and which is soon joined by Fitt's raspy one. 'Fitt, I don't know what you're laughing about, you have a clump of snowballs hanging from your chin.'

'And you have a cut above your eye,' Sonja hollers to me. 'Fitt, that last one was a corker. Aleks, are you going to heal that yourself or do you want me to? I think we can pull off looking like we've ridden through a snowstorm, because we have. You can't pull that off though, the blood trickling down your face makes you look a little sinister.'

*I'm on it. This multiskilling thing is easy once you get your head around it, isn't it? It's hard to believe there was a time when glass-singing was all I could do.* I heal the cut and wipe the blood from my face with a handkerchief. *There. Better?*

Fitt and Sonja both nod and Fitt gives me a thumbs up.

*Great.*

*Just in time,* Sonja warns me. *Face forward.*

I turn back towards Bigwood and make out a crowd of heavily-garbed villagers waiting by the closest cottages, currently containing only a dozen or so people but about to gain rapidly in

size judging by the number running along the street to join it. I am
Aware of the villagers' excitement at the sight of the horses, Sonja
and me, then, as we get closer, their fear, horror and revulsion at
the sight of Fitt astride Flame.

I understand. Having been so scared of the Woeful, as I used
to think of the Kindred, I could hardly bear to look at Fitt in the
early days of knowing her since every time I did, terror gripped
my heart so hard I thought it would stop. And here she is, her
talons and fangs no less lethal than they've always been, looking
even larger than normal as a result of sitting astride Flame, and
actually a little scarier now that she has snow and ice clinging to
every inch of her wiry fur.

I sense the enthusiasm for the chance to achieve Awareness
that has lingered with most of the villagers since their visit from
the Herald – himself Aware as a result of the Kindreds' help – who
passed through here last week with the news that a Kindred
Horse-Bonded would soon be on her way to help them attain it.
But I also pick up from them the amount of time it took the Herald
to convince them to give the visiting Kindred as warm a welcome
as they would any other Horse-Bonded, and that regardless, they
are every bit as scared as they expected to be.

I know only too well, from very personal experience, how
often and how easily fear is expressed as hate, and I recognise that
energy now rapidly developing in the crowd that awaits us. Fitt is
Aware of it too. I sense Bright acceding to Sonja's request to pick
up his pace so that they pass Fitt and Flame, and settle into place
next to Nexus and me.

*There's no need to shield me,* Fitt remarks, her thought weaker
than usual.

*There's every need,* I reply firmly. When Fitt and the other
Kindred arrived at Rockwood to the same reaction she is evoking
here, its ferocity was distributed amongst all of them whilst also

being dissipated by the nine horses and eight humans who accompanied them. Here, the villagers' hate is being directed solely at her and I can feel how much its ferocity has shaken her. Sonja and I are here to help her as much as we possibly can, and at this moment in time, that means giving her a few minutes to collect herself.

Dazzling white light bursts from Sonja towards the waiting villagers and as always, I am proud of her strength; there aren't many who can affect a crowd as large as the one that is continuing to swell before us. Nevertheless, I add my light to hers – I've learnt that there's no such thing as too much love.

It works. The intensity of the villagers' animosity towards Fitt wanes as our light settles around them and we block her from their sight. Where Fitt had braced herself against the force of feeling directed at her, I now sense her relaxing and focusing everything of herself on being in balance with her horse and within herself. My relief is matched by Sonja's; being Kindred, Flame can't help but broadcast aspects of herself to humans when she looks at them and it is imperative that it is her wish to help them, and her confidence that she can, that are available for them to pick up on and not her self-doubt.

Nexus and Bright move apart slightly so that Fitt and Flame are again visible. As one, the horses pick up on our intention and draw themselves up out of the snow so that rather than moving through it, we feel as if they are dancing atop it. There is a collective gasp from our audience as the six of us power towards them at a trot. I sense their confusion as they find themselves staring in wonder at the sight before them, which includes the one towards whom only moments before, they felt so much fear and animosity. Our horses glide to a halt in front of the villagers, disturbing not so much as a single snowflake from the narrow band of snow that separates them from us.

'Greetings, villagers of Bigwood,' I call loudly, the wind taking my voice to them so that even those at the back hear me. 'I'm Aleks and this Nexus, also known as the love of my life.' I wink at Sonja, who shakes her head and grins as I hold my hand out towards her and Fitt. 'This is Sonja and her Bond-Partner, Bright, and we all have the privilege to be accompanying Fitt and her Bond-Partner, Flame.'

I lower my hand to direct my audience's attention to the tall, chestnut mare with four white legs who stands patiently between Bright and Nexus, ears pricked but eyes mellow as her warm breath leaves her nostrils in soft, wispy clouds. I choose my next words carefully. 'Sonja and I came across Flame last year when we were travelling with Amarilla Nixon and her Bond-Partner, Infinity.' Many glances are exchanged at the mention of two whose names are so well known in these parts. 'Flame was horribly injured and actually, we weren't sure if she'd survive. None of us could understand how she'd borne the pain she was in for as long as she had, or how she'd managed to drag herself a considerable distance in order to put herself in our path. But then we realised exactly how and why she'd done those things; there was something she wanted to do and she was determined not to die until she'd done it. Want to know what it was?'

The villagers nod uncertainly as they look between Flame and me, to a one carefully avoiding looking at Fitt.

'She wanted to find the Kindred who would help her to heal, and she wanted to bond with that Kindred and help her to heal in return so that the two of them could help all of us.'

I pause to let my words sink in, then relax as I sense Sonja's intentions. She would have us allow our light to fade so that the villagers can begin to accept Fitt without its influence, and she would speak.

I allow my light to slowly wane in concert with hers as she

calls out, 'I used to think I knew what courage was. Soon after meeting Fitt and Flame, I realised that I had no idea. This horse…' She swallows and looks at Flame with tears in her eyes. 'This horse endured unimaginable pain in order to find us and her Bond-Partner. She was brave enough to put aside all of her instincts to flee one of those she and her kind had always seen as a predator, and invite Fitt to sit on her back. This beautiful Kindred,' she continues, looking up at Fitt, 'was gentle enough, kind enough, for Flame to be able to accept her as her Bond-Partner despite her heritage.' She diverts her gaze to the villagers, making eye contact with as many of them as she can. 'Fitt and Flame were willing to risk everything, and I mean everything, to help us convince the Kindred of Shady Mountain that we humans are capable of relinquishing our fears and evolving. As a result, the vast proportion of the villagers of Rockwood, as I know you already know, are now Aware and have welcomed Fitt's family and friends – Aleks's and my friends – to live among them.

'Fitt and Flame are here with us now to help you to Awareness. Fitt has very kindly been avoiding looking directly at any of you, to give you the time to adjust to her presence.' Fitt lifts her eyes from Flame's mane in front of her, to those who stand in rapt silence before the six of us. 'Now that she's looking at you, you'll be able to feel who she is if you allow yourselves to. You'll know of her kindness and her determination to help you all – you'll know exactly why Aleks and I love her so much. Why Flame loves her so much.'

Sonja glances across at me, her question as obvious in her eyes as in her thought. I give the barest of nods. She and I have done all we can. Now it's up to Fitt.

FOUR

# Fitt

*I* glance at each of the villagers in turn, knowing instantly which of them are now relaxed enough to perceive the broadcast of myself carried by my gaze. Of the hundreds standing on the icy cobbles before us, all wrapped from head to toe against the cold so that only their eyes show, just seventeen know my true nature and intentions. The rest bombard me with revulsion as my eyes rest upon them. Their revulsion only grows as they scrutinise my body, along with their fear as they imagine the uses to which I have put it, and their anger and hate as they remember all of the times they have been forced to travel hastily through woodland for fear of being preyed upon by my kind.

I find myself sympathising with both their fear and their anger, for both are warranted – as is their revulsion.

*No they aren't, Fitt,* Sonja tells me calmly.

I'm an abomination, just like my ancestors were always taught they were. When I see myself through the eyes of those before me, I see it.

*Fitt, centre yourself.* Aleks takes hold of my arm and gently squeezes it. *FITT! You're past all that stuff. Focus on who you are and why you're here, come on, you can do it.* His belief in me accompanies his thought, but the villagers' fear and loathing are stronger and when they funnel them into words which they hurl in my direction, I am almost knocked from Flame's back.

'Those fangs and talons aren't coming anywhere near my children,' an adult female shouts, her voice whipped away by the wind even as the thought behind it pierces my heart. A cacophony of thoughts join it as all of the spoken words they evoke are likewise taken by the wind.

*You can call yourself a Kindred all you like, but you're a Woeful. A big, aggressive, dangerous Woeful.*

*One of your lot killed my donkeys three summers ago, and you think you can just ride in here on a horse you've probably terrified into carrying you, and we'll welcome you with open arms?*

*Go back to your kind and take them away from Rockwood, away from good, honest people.*

Their thoughts jumble together in my mind, tangling with my own as I fight to stay on my horse. Why am I here? Why did I think I could help these humans? Who was I to think I would be strong enough to overcome their fear of me when it took Amarilla's bond with her sister to even begin the process in Rockwood? They'll never accept me. I avert my eyes from them and see instead my memories of the humans of The Old throwing stones and shouting taunts at my ancestors.

*You forgave them.* The thought is faint yet weaves its way determinedly between all of the other thoughts and images currently assailing my mind. And it is warm and loving where everything else is cold and hurtful.

*FLAME????????* Everything else – everyone else – melts

away. *How are you doing this? Why are you using thoughts to communicate with me?*

*It has become necessary now that you are experiencing the level of challenge that only humans can evoke. Focus your mind on my thoughts as strongly as you evaded my influence. Remember the energy of forgiveness and unfurl yourself.*

I blink. I am still astride the warmth that is Flame, but my shoulders are hunched and not as a result of the wind that continues to batter at my back; I once more bear upon them the weight of my ancestors' torment. The torment that I realised some time ago, with Flame's help, had only as much power over me as I was willing to give it. I summon the energy of forgiveness and know again that no wrong was done to my ancestors by the humans of The Old because in truth, there is no right and wrong, just the learning of souls.

My eyes and ears focus once again on my surroundings, and I find that Bright and Nexus have moved in front of Flame and me again, their riders gesticulating animatedly at those who can barely hear them. I feel calmer, yet not at peace as the act of forgiving has always left me in the past.

*You yet protect yourself from that which cannot harm you.* Flame's thought shocks me all over again as it draws my attention to my shoulders.

While no longer hunched under the weight of the past, they are nevertheless curled over and around my chest. Around my heart, I realise, which hurts with the pain of rejection that I expected and for which I tried to prepare practically, but for which I neglected to prepare in the way that matters.

Flame shifts beneath me and I move instinctively in response. *Balancing your mind is as simple as balancing your body. This you know,* she tells me.

And I remember that I do. We Are Flame. I will forgive those who fear and are disgusted by me, for their feelings are part of their evolution and nothing more; no affront, no attack on me exists. My heart throbs in protest but I am firmly with my Bond-Partner. If I can forgive the hurt of generations that was held within the Kindred collective consciousness, I can forgive that which is before me now.

Most of the hurt lifts from my heart and dissipates… yet some of it lingers, clutching at me with such strength that I can't seem to release it. I focus on the fear and revulsion still being directed at me and see them again for what they really are. I fully expect the remainder of the hurt still lodged in my heart to shift – but in vain.

*It is more difficult to forgive trauma that is personal than that which was suffered by your ancestors,* Flame advises me. *And more difficult still to dismiss energy that highlights an insecurity within you.*

I focus on her thought and sway atop her slightly as I realise to what she is referring; I am like a leaf blown about by the wind when I'm surrounded by those who are sure that I am exactly as their fear causes them to see me.

*The issue does not arise when you are surrounded by those who know who you are and see you as such,* Flame confirms. *When you can be sure of yourself regardless of circumstance then you will be all the more potent for it.*

*When I can be sure of myself,* I repeat and wince.

I want to turn around and escape with Flame back to the trees where we'll be out of sight and out of mind – where I'll have the space to sort out what I've discovered about myself. We could do it too; harsh as the weather is, it was just as bad at times when we were travelling to Rockwood, and it troubled us little.

*You need not evade that which concerns you,* Flame informs me. *Merely embrace whom you know yourself to be and forgive any energy that disputes it. The answer is always the same regardless of the question.*

Her warmth and determination are as strong as ever despite mine having failed at the first challenge. She is tired and hungry yet despite her discomfort, she has found a way to order her feelings into thoughts that can reach the part of my mind that hungers to be accepted by those around me.

I feel love for my horse with all of my heart... and the hurt that clung to it is blasted to nothing. I am Aware of Flame's approval as my love for her bursts out of me, to those in front of us. She gathers herself and nudges Nexus and Bright to either side so that she can pass between them.

*Well that's a bit more like it, go Fitt!* Aleks grins at me as we power past him and his Bond-Partner.

Sonja sends a short burst of light to me in recognition of that which blazes from my heart as Flame and I approach the nearest members of the crowd. Our love and warmth settle over everyone who hates me as Flame causes them to part before us. Their taunts and insults cease as they watch us both in confused amazement.

Flame halts in front of a diminutive adult female dressed from head to toe in blue. Her tiny, gloved hand appears from beneath her cloak and tentatively reaches out to my horse, who sniffs it politely before stretching out her neck so that she can sniff and then nuzzle the human's shoulder. The human's eyes crinkle at their corners as she smiles behind her scarf, then lift to meet mine.

I peruse everything I know about her in my Awareness and focus on the aspects of myself that are similar so that my energy resonates with hers. Her eyes widen as she senses our connection, then widen further as she senses more from me than that which she picked up from my broadcast of myself. I reveal all that I am and welcome the touch of her mind as she reaches out for yet more. I guide her to Flame and she staggers backward in astonishment.

An adult male puts his arm around her and hollers to me, 'What have you done to her?'

The female shakes him off and steps back to Flame and me. She reaches up to my horse and gently rests a hand on her neck, then steps closer and lays her other hand on my calf, her eyes full of tears. *I'm so sorry.*

*You have nothing to be sorry for,* I reply. *You're Aware of me now, you know that's how I feel.*

She steps back again in surprise that I not only heard her thought but replied with my own, then pulls her scarf from her face and laughs with delight. *I am! I'm Aware of you!*

I guide her fledgling Awareness to Sonja, who smiles and waves. *We thank you for your courage and openness, Shefali. Do you think you could organise lodging for the six of us now, before we all freeze to death?* The humour accompanying her thought doesn't take away from the fact that her request is genuine.

Shefali puts both of her hands to her head. *I'm such an idiot. Of course! Fitt, you and Flame will stay with me. Everyone, who'll host Sonja and Aleks and their horses? Curse the clouds, they can't hear me, of course they can't. They're all looking at me as if I'm nuts. Flaming lanterns, Nostan's terrified of you, Fitt, oooh and he's scared of spiders too. How funny, look at him, big strong man he is and scared of spiders! He loves his wife and children though, that's why he's so scared of you, not for himself but for his family. And Jaze is…*

*Shefali, focus on me,* I instruct her. *Shefali. SHEFALI!*

She stops mid-thought and looks at me in surprise. I smile at her and sense the collective gasp that the wind whips from my ears, amid a wave of horror at what the crowd perceives to be my snarl.

Shefali senses my momentary hurt before Flame shifts beneath me, reminding me how to render it harmless. She turns to those around her, the fury on her face obvious enough to reach those who can't hear her as she yells, 'Fitt's smiling, you idiots. She's so, so brave, coming here to try and help us all, so don't you upset her. Any of you.' Her fellow villagers shrink back from her pointed finger in surprise. 'Fitt and Flame will be my guests, so you lot,' she jabs her finger at those closest to her, 'can sort out who's going to invite Aleks and Sonja and their horses to stay before they all freeze solid where they stand.'

It's all I can do to stop myself laughing out loud as the villagers look in stunned amazement between Shefali and me. I am Aware that the Shefali they know is quiet and unassuming, quite the opposite of the female before them now whose sense of Flame has put fire in her belly.

*Come on, Fitt, follow me,* she tells me. *Once that lot haven't got anyone to gawp at, they'll fall over themselves offering your friends lodging.*

She puts her arms out in front of her and parts those blocking her path, slapping the arms of those who are slow to move, so that the way clears for Flame and me to follow her. She shakes her head and holds her hands up at those who try to protest at her actions, actually pushing an adult male who tries to stand in her way with his feet apart and arms crossed. 'When you understand what's going on here, you're going to feel like such a fool, Jaze,' she tells him angrily, her face so close to his that he can't mistake either her words or her wrath.

He stands aside in surprise, his eyebrows raised almost under his hat as he watches her stalk past him. He lowers them into a scowl as he looks up at me. At one with the horse who is moving so powerfully yet so lightly beneath me, I am able to deny his distaste the opportunity to reach my heart.

# FIVE

## Sonja

_T_he villagers watch Fitt and Flame following Shefali down the street. Fitt remains astride her horse both in order to continue receiving her help, and to avoid alarming the crowd further by dismounting. It isn't until they turn between two cottages, for the paddocks behind, that the spell cast by the three of them breaks and the villagers turn back to Aleks and me.

We both relax as the atmosphere lifts and we no longer have to work at remaining centred in the face of our irritation at how these people were treating our friend. We dismount as the crowd surges towards us, all of its members eager to welcome to their village Horse-Bonded who fit their idea of normality.

I accept the outstretched hand of the first to reach me, a woman who leans in close so that I can hear her. 'It's lovely to meet you, Sonja, I'm Tosca. Will you and your horse come and stay with me and my family?'

I am Aware that although she would have offered her hospitality anyway, desperation accompanies her invitation; she thinks I can offer her protection from Fitt. I feel like refusing her, but Bright nudges my mind as he tends to when I need reminding of that which I already know. I balance my exasperation with my Awareness of Tosca's genuine fear, and remember that Aleks and I aren't just here to help Fitt, but also the people of Bigwood.

I shake the hand she is holding out to me. 'Thank you, that's very kind. You have a shelter big enough for Bright?'

She nods enthusiastically. 'A huge one, we have sheep. He'll be alright sharing with them?'

'He will, thank you.' I shake more gloved hands whilst checking in with Aleks. *Are you sorted?*

*Yep, Nexus and I'll be next door to where Fitt and Flame are staying. Neem, here, practically fell over himself to get to me first, he thinks he needs my protection. It'll be amusing to see their faces when they all become Aware and realise how silly they've been, won't it?*

*Almost as funny as when it happened to you.* I grin over my shoulder at him as I begin to follow Tosca to her home. He sticks his tongue out at me. *Careful,* I warn him, *it'll freeze like that.*

*On a day like today, that's no jest. See you when I see you, Sonn.*

I continue shaking hands as Tosca, Bright and I make our way through the crowd. Bright sniffs most of the hands before they are offered to me, then accepts strokes of his neck as he passes by.

I call out, 'Anyone who wants Bright's counsel, come along and see us in the morning.' It's pretty pointless, not just because neither I nor anyone else can hear my voice, but because as villagers of The New, they all know that visiting Horse-Bonded always make themselves available to those wanting help once they've had a chance to settle their horses and themselves into their lodgings.

I wonder if any of them will visit Fitt and Flame, and instantly know that while there are some who will, the majority will be tougher for Fitt to reach. My thought moves my friend to the forefront of my Awareness; she and Shefali are busy rigging up a hay rack for Flame, who is currently quenching her thirst.

*We are well, thank you, my friend,* Fitt tells me.

*I'm glad. Let me know if you need any help with anything, won't you?*

*You've done what was necessary, now you and Aleks should put all of your efforts into those who will come to your horses for counsel, like we agreed. Flame is all the help I need.* Fitt's thought rings with determination but she can't hide the trepidation she also feels. She blasts it away with more determination as soon as my perusal of it brings it to her attention. *We Are Flame,* she asserts to herself as much as to me.

I am relieved to find that while Aleks is being hosted in the cottage on one side of Shefali's, Tosca and her family occupy the one on the other. I suppose I shouldn't be surprised that fear gave Tosca's and Neem's legs the strength to reach the two of us first, and I'm glad it did even though it isn't the two of them or their families over whom Aleks and I both feel protective.

Flame whinnies an echoing welcome as she senses Bright enter the shelter that backs onto hers. He whinnies back and I sense, rather than hear, Nexus's reply from two paddocks over. I almost overbalance as I enter the shelter behind my horse, so used am I to having to lean into the wind that I miss its support when beyond its reach.

'Phew, this is better, isn't it?' Tosca says, pulling her scarf below her chin, and her hood back from her cropped blond hair, through which she runs gloved fingers. She nods to the far half of the shelter where sheep are nestled in the deep straw bed. 'They don't take up too much space, Bright should have plenty of room to lie down. There's a water trough over there. One of us comes out every few hours to break the ice.'

'It's great, thank you,' I reply as Bright heads for a row of low-hung hay racks all brimming with hay. I hurry after him, remove his saddle and rub his coat with my hands where the saddle and girth have flattened it. I check him all over with my hands and mind before pulling a hoof pick from one of my saddlebags and chipping at the compacted ice in his feet. When I'm satisfied that my horse is comfortable and has everything he needs, I hoist my saddlebags onto my shoulders, take my saddle into my arms and turn to where Tosca is waiting for me.

Immediately, I lower my bags and saddle back down to the straw. My hands and feet will have to wait a bit longer to defrost – Tosca is in need of Bright's counsel now.

She inclines her head towards her cottage. 'Come on, you must be desperate to get in the warm.'

I smile at her. 'It's okay. Ask Bright what you'd like to know.'

'Now? Are you sure? I guess I could ask him and then you could tell me his reply once we're inside?'

It's a tempting proposition, but not how we do things; it's not how the process works. While the people of The New trust us Horse-Bonded, we are still human, like them. As descendants of the Ancients, all of whom followed their intuition and left the known for the unknown, they are all sensitive enough to feel reassured by the calm strength of a horse's physical presence, and as such are in a better place to accept their counsel when they are near the source of it, however difficult it might be to hear.

'We'll stay out here until you have the information you need,' I tell her. 'Go ahead.'

Tosca shuffles through the straw until she is standing next to me. 'I'd like Bright's reassurance that my children are safe with that...' She coughs nervously. 'With, um, with who's staying next door. I know you trust her but I'm sorry, I'd really like to hear from Bright that we're all safe, and ask how I'm supposed to sleep at night knowing there's a Woe… I mean knowing she's there.' She avoids looking at me and shifts from one foot to the other and back again.

Bright turns to look at Tosca, his eyes soft and knowing. *You need no reassurance. Allow yourself to admit that it is not She Who Is Flame whom you fear so much as the change she represents.*

I pass on his advice to Tosca, as always very sure to phrase it exactly as I perceived it in my mind.

'I… what?' Tosca stands open mouthed as she stares between Bright – who returns his attention to the hay rack – and me.

'Just let his counsel sink in, don't try to fight it,' I advise, knowing from long experience that my advice is as sound as my Bond-Partner's. 'I'll be over there if you need me.'

I settle myself on a bale of straw lining the shelter wall and, cold as I am, take my own advice and let Bright's earlier counsel sink in once again. I release the judgement I was about to make about the cold being a curse, and find myself merely cold instead of cold and miserable.

Several times, Tosca glances at Bright – who continues to munch his hay contentedly – as if she will speak, then frowns and returns her gaze to the straw at her feet. Eventually, she says, 'But we've always been taught to fear the Woeful – sorry, the Kindred. And now there's one here. Fitt's here, and she wants to teach us all how to know what everyone else is thinking and feeling? How can it be a good thing for us all to know that about one another?'

I notice the relative ease with which she can now speak my friend's name, and smile to myself. As always, my horse knew exactly which words I needed to say in order to simplify things, thereby gaining the biggest impact in the shortest time.

*Only humans are capable of creating complications where there are none,* my horse observes, and my smile turns to a grimace as I remember how capable I still am of getting in my own way.

When I sense Tosca's eyes on me, I hold my hands up to her. 'Sorry, Bright was just highlighting something for me. He's now telling me his answer to your question. He suggests that you employ the same strategy the humans of The New always have when confronted with something new.'

Tosca looks blankly at me.

'Use your intuition. Feel your way. Don't think about what's happening, trust how you feel about it deep inside.'

Bright shifts his hind end towards her and she takes the hint, murmuring, 'Right, well, I suppose I'd better let that sink in as well then.'

I get to my feet and find that I can't feel them. I try to grasp my saddle bags but my fingers refuse to curl around the straps.

Tosca hurries over. 'I'm so sorry, look at you, you can barely move and your lips are turning blue. Here, I'll take those. Let's get you inside.' She hooks both bags over one shoulder and puts her other arm around me as I pick up my saddle. She pulls me close and guides me out of the shelter. When the wind catches us, she helps me through the snow towards the back door of her cottage. She lets go of me momentarily while she opens the door, then pushes me in ahead of her and slams the door, leaning back on it to make sure the catch has caught.

A warm wave of air caresses my face and my eyelids suddenly feel heavy. I sway on the spot and put a hand out to the grey stone wall to steady myself.

Tosca takes my saddle from me and lowers it to an enormous flagstone by the door, then grips my arms and propels me in front of her along a grey stone-walled hallway to a large, untidy kitchen. She deposits me on a chair at a table covered with dirty plates, and hurries to a doorway at the far end of the room. When she opens the door, the sounds of children laughing, shouting and running erupt into the room.

Tosca calls out, 'Semina, Grantham, get yourselves down here, please.' She waits until footsteps begin to pound the stairs, then hurries to the stove where she pours water from a kettle into a teapot, adding tea leaves before placing it on the table in front of me along with a mug, a tea strainer and a jar of honey. I can't find the energy to do anything other than watch her.

A girl and a boy, both in their mid teens and as dark in complexion as their mother is fair, come hurtling into the kitchen. They skid to a stop when they see me, and their faces light up.

The girl says, 'You brought a Horse-Bonded home, Mum? You actually brought one of them home? That's soooooooooo amazing!'

'Sonja, meet my eldest two children,' Tosca says. 'Semmy and Grant are about to demonstrate how quickly they can clear the table and wash the dishes, which they were supposed to have organised my younger children to do before any of them left the kitchen.' She turns to the teenagers. 'Semmy, Grant, meet Sonja. She and her Bond-Partner, Bright, will be staying with us for a while. Bright is happily eating hay out with the sheep, but Sonja's on the verge of hypothermia and needs peace, quiet, a hot bath, a decent meal, and a good sleep, in that order. I'll sort the meal out but I'd like you both to organise everything else, please.'

'Oooooh, can we see Bright first?' Semmy asks.

'He's had a difficult and strenuous journey from Rockwood in this weather, and needs to rest,' her mother replies. 'You can see him when Sonja says you can and not before. The sooner she's recovered from her travels, the sooner she'll be in a position to grant you your request.'

Grant turns to me. 'What about the Woeful? Is it here in

Bigwood?' His voice drops to a whisper. 'Has it killed anyone yet?'

I can't prevent my gaze hardening as I look up into his dark, suddenly scared eyes, but manage to recover quickly. 'She's a Kindred, not a Woeful,' I explain, 'and her name is Fitt. She's Horse-Bonded, just like me, and her horse, Flame, will enjoy meeting you every bit as much as Bright will. You know, when I first met Fitt, it was because she needed help. She was hungry because she couldn't hunt for herself. Do you want to know why that was?'

Grant, Semmy and Tosca all nod their heads in unison, Tosca's focus on me as avid as her children's.

'Because like all Kindred, she can't abide suffering. She didn't trust herself to make her kills clean, so she wouldn't kill at all until a friend of mine taught her to hunt with a bow and arrows, like we do. Shall I tell you the only time she's ever killed anything with her talons and fangs?'

All three nod again and lean closer to me.

'She was forced to take the life of a wild cat to stop it killing Flame.'

Tosca covers her mouth with both hands and Semmy squeaks.

Grant punches the air and says, 'Awesome!'

I nod. 'It was. Flame was trying to get to Fitt in order to bond with her and she was almost there when the wild cat caught her scent. She was lame and couldn't run at full speed, so the cat caught up with her and was just about to take her down when Fitt put a stop to it.'

'Flame was trying to get to Fitt?' Semmy says. 'But that's not how it works, we've learnt about it at school. A horse tugs the person they've chosen as a Bond-Partner and that person goes to find the horse. It's called going on a quest and the village holds a Quest Ceremony before they leave.'

Grant throws his hands up in the air. 'She knows that, stupid, she's Horse-Bonded.'

Tosca puts her hands on her hips. '"She" is called Sonja, Grant, and you'll apologise to your sister immediately for calling her stupid.'

Grant glances at Semmy and mutters, 'Sorry,' before reverting his attention to me, his eyes shining. 'So, why did Flame go to find Fitt when it should have been the other way around?'

I smile, as much at the heat now slowly spreading through my body as at Grant's enthusiasm having replaced his fear of my friend. 'Because Fitt would never have approached Flame. She knew she was injured and scared and she didn't want to frighten her even more, so she kept out of sight and waited until Flame was ready to approach her instead. Then they bonded and Fitt helped Flame to heal. Can you imagine how hard it is to want so much to help someone, and not be able to because they're scared of you?'

Semmy and Grant both stare uncomprehendingly at me but Tosca begins to nod slowly. She turns to her children. 'Do you remember when Kuli was screaming because a wasp had stung her, and we all went running out to the garden to help her? It was horrible, wasn't it, seeing her in so much pain. What would we have done if she'd been scared of us? Too scared to let you carry her inside, Grant, and too scared to let you bathe her hand like you did, Sem, while I ran for the Herbalist?'

Both of the teenagers frown.

'That's what it was like for Fitt when she was waiting for Flame to trust her,' I say. 'And it's what it's like for her now she's here in Bigwood. She wants so much to help all of you here, and she's waiting for you to realise you have no reason to be afraid of her. She might look different from you and me, but she's the same inside. She loves her horse, her family and friends, and she'd give her life for any one of us.' I can't help but send Fitt a wave of love as I remember that she already has done.

Her attention flickers to me and she immediately absorbs everything I've said about her. Her spirits lift as she senses the shift occurring within the three who are hanging on to every word I've said.

I warn her, *Brace yourself, there'll be at least two children racing your way as soon as they're allowed to.*

*I will welcome them.* Her thought is as warm as her heart.

'Can we go and see Fitt and Flame now?' Grant says and Semmy nods enthusiastically.

'No one is going anywhere,' Tosca says firmly, 'until their chores are done and the new arrivals – all of them – have had the care and rest they need.'

Semmy and Grant roll their eyes, and Semmy sighs as she says to her brother, 'You start clearing the table, I'll get the others running a bath and making up the spare bed.' She goes to the door and yells instructions up the stairs until the shrieking stops and she's satisfied that the sound of running feet means her siblings are acceding to her demands. Then she hurries to the sink and begins filling it with hot, soapy water.

Tosca smiles at me as she pours tea into my mug. 'We'll have you feeling better in no time.'

I manage a weary smile in response. 'I know you're worried about everyone knowing your thoughts, and about what you'll find out if you can be Aware of theirs, but I never told you what I need right now, or that Bright needs rest. Awareness is just a natural extension of the intuition you already have, you know.'

She looks at me thoughtfully. 'I've had counsel from horses who've visited with their Bond-Partners in the past, but I've never hosted a Horse-Bonded before. Is it always like this? Do you always have this much impact on those you spend more time with?'

'Come to think of it, no. Things are changing quickly though. I've changed so much since I last visited any villages, I barely recognise myself, and thanks to Bright and Fitt, I made another change just earlier on today.'

Tosca chews on her lip as she turns away from me and heads back to the stove.

# SIX

## Aleks

*N*ow I know that Sonja's enjoying a hot bath, and Fitt a decent meal, I can give Neem and his wife and son all of my attention instead of most of it.

Neem puts a steaming mug of spiced wine down on the table in front of me. 'Get that down you and then try again to convince me why I should not only be happy there's a monster staying next door, but that it's a good idea for me to allow it into my head,' he snaps, his trembling hand belying his attempt at aggression.

If I weren't Aware exactly why he's speaking to me without the respect usually afforded the Horse-Bonded, I would be surprised by his tone and annoyed at his references to my friend. Instead, I reply in as mild a tone as I can manage, 'Are you sure you want me to repeat myself for, what will it be now, the fourth time? It will save a lot of time if you just ask Nexus?'

Neem sits down opposite me and stares into his own mug of wine. He's still not ready to ask the one whose answer he knows he can't dispute. His wife grasps her mug so tightly, her fingers are white despite the heat radiating from it.

'How are you feeling about Fitt being here, Fennel?' I ask her, knowing full well but trying to get her to break the terrified silence she has maintained since the four of us entered their cottage.

'I... that is... I...' She glances at Neem and then takes a hurried sip of her wine. I wince as I sense it burning her throat, but she gulps it down and then stares at the remainder, willing it to cool so she can down the lot.

'Malek?' I'm hoping for an advance on the glum staring that the couple's son has employed so far.

'She scares me,' he replies.

'You feel scared of her, there's a world of difference,' I point out cheerfully.

Neem scowls at me, his thick, black eyebrows meeting in the middle of his forehead. 'Which is?'

'If Fitt had hidden down a side street and leapt out on Malek unexpectedly so that his body instinctively went into fight or flight mode, then I would have agreed that she scared him. What she actually did was find the courage to ride to this village in appalling conditions, approach it in such a way as to make it as obvious as possible that she's a friend, help one of your number to Awareness and then take herself off to give the rest of you time to accustom yourselves to her presence. If anyone chooses to feel scared of her, that's down to them and no one else.'

Neem glares at me and thumps his mug down on the table.

I lift both of my hands in surrender. 'You're angry with me for saying it like it is, I get it.' I smile to myself in the knowledge that if Levitsson were here, he would be proud of me.

'You also clearly think that bringing a Woeful among us is funny,' Neem snarls.

'Certainly not from Fitt's point of view. Looking at us humans from the point of view of one of my other Kindred friends is definitely amusing though, you see what we do is this; we behave in one way to hide the fact that we actually feel another. You're pretending to be angry because it's easier than feeling scared and helpless. You can choose another option though, a much easier one. If you want to, that is?'

Neem continues to glower at me. Fennel's eyes dart between us both and she jumps when Malek asks, 'What's the easier option?'

I flick my eyebrows up and down at him, daring him to believe me. 'Trust.'

Neem sits back in his chair and folds his arms. 'Trust a Woeful? When my whole life, I've been told to avoid them like a wasp's nest, and with good reason?'

'I was meaning trust yourself, actually, but for now, trusting Nexus will be a start. Haven't you also been told your whole life to trust the horses? They've always counselled against harming those we used to regard as woeful and aggressive but now know to be our friends – our kindred. Nine horses, including Nexus, happily took their Bond-Partners, including me, straight into the heart of a Kindred community, knowing that the descendants of those bred to enforce the madness of The Old would be the making of The New. And three of those horses are here in Bigwood to help you all accept that's the case.

'I know how it feels to be so frightened as to become irrational, in fact I'm a past master at it. There was a time when I didn't trust my fellow Horse-Bonded and I certainly didn't trust Fitt. But I never stopped trusting Nexus, and you shouldn't either.'

Fennel finally releases her mug, and stretches trembling hands out to take hold of those of her husband and son. 'Aleks is right. Without the horses, The New wouldn't exist. We wouldn't even be here. We've always listened to their counsel before and they've never failed us. Any of us.' She looks at me, her hazel eyes desperate. 'You're wet, cold and tired, Aleks, I see that and I'm sorry, but could we please go out to ask Nexus for her counsel now? If we wait, I'll lose my nerve.'

I'm at the back door in an instant. 'Give a Horse-Bonded the chance to be with his Bond-Partner and he'll take it. Come on, she's waiting for us.'

Fennel and Malek both stand but Neem remains seated, refusing to allow his wife to even lift his hand from the table. Fennel murmurs, 'Nexus is waiting, love.'

Neem glares at her for a while, then his shoulders sag and his eyes soften. But then his fear fights for resurrection. He braces his shoulders and says to me, 'Can't you just tell us her counsel? You can ask her for it from here, can't you?'

'So can you, but if she wanted to do it that way, she wouldn't be waiting for you to go and see her,' I reply.

'Come on, Dad,' Malek says. 'Fitt won't be out there...' He glances at me and I shake my head in confirmation. 'Just Nexus.'

Neem rolls his eyes and gets to his feet, grumbling to himself, 'Going out in this weather to ask advice about a Woeful when we already know what we should do, when we should already be doing it, is just idiotic. If Nexus was so desperate to tell us different, she'd have done it when we saw her to the shelter, not waited until we've just got warm and then dragged us back out into the cold. This is total madness...' His words are cut off from me as I step out into the ferocious wind.

I wrap my arms around myself in self-defence, but then remember. The wind, the snow, the cold – none of them are good or bad, they just are. I am Aware of Sonja's smile as if she were right in front of me rather than languishing in the bath.

*It makes life so much easier, doesn't it,* she observes.

*Absolutely, and I think the more we do it, the more naturally it'll come,* I reply, Aware that Neem is now trying to keep up with his wife and son as they hurry to keep up with me.

*I'm hoping the same will apply to forgiving people for their treatment of Fitt, that's harder, isn't it?*

*Not for me, I remember feeling exactly as they all do. There's definitely something to be said for having floundered for so long at rock bottom. Enjoy your bath, and the meal I can smell through your senses – turn that off somehow, will you? It's just mean.*

*Dismiss it as neither good nor bad, Aleks, the more you do it, the easier it'll come.*

I chuckle at the mischievousness that accompanies her thought, then as I step into the shelter that Nexus is sharing with four donkeys, I lose all sense of anything except for my horse. I move straight towards her in the dim light, Aware that her larger than average, darker than average and, I dare to venture, gentler than average eyes are fixed on me as her slender grey body gradually becomes visible in the gloom.

As always when I am in her physical presence, her kindness and the tenderness she feels towards me are magnified, and I congratulate myself for what must be the millionth time on having had the good sense to agree to incarnate this time around with her as my Bond-Partner. I can cope with anything Neem or anyone else throws at me, but that doesn't mean that the love and acceptance I feel from my horse are any less a balm to my soul.

Neem's voice booms into the shelter. 'Let's get this over with, then.'

If Levittson were here, he wouldn't be able to stop himself pointing out that Neem has progressed well from anger and aggression to the false bravado that is the final layer beneath which his fear is lurking. Our visit to Nexus is perfectly timed.

I turn and then wince momentarily at light emanating from a

lantern that Fennel is holding before her. 'Come on over,' I tell the family, and grin at Malek as he hurries to my side.

Fennel follows her son, then turns to where Neem appears to have taken root by the doorway, the sight of my horse in the lanternlight having robbed him of everything except true emotion. Perfect.

'What would you like to ask Nexus, Neem?' I ask him.

He opens and closes his mouth several times before whispering, 'How do I know for certain that the Woeful won't kill me, my wife and son?'

Nexus leaves the hay rack she has been steadily emptying since her arrival, and weaves her way slowly between the donkeys – all of whom are resting a hind leg while snoozing – to stand in front of Neem. He takes a step backward and looks as if he will turn and run from her, but then relaxes as she blows warm breath into the crook of his neck.

*It will serve him to consider why he has assumed it a possibility that she will.*

I relay Nexus's counsel to Neem, who looks past her to me, his face lined with fury. 'Because we've always been told that's what they do. Just because she's made some horses and Horse-Bonded trust her, doesn't mean she might not still have it in her to kill us.'

'We've never been told that Woeful kill humans, only that they might injure us while trying to kill our donkeys or steal from us,' Fennel says gently.

'Okay, so the donkeys then. How do we know she won't kill them, mortally wounding us in the process?' Neem says breathlessly.

'Nexus advises you to put into words everything you know of Fitt's true nature,' I say, smiling at my horse as she continues to breathe everything she is into Neem.

'Well, she's huge, for a start, and those fangs and talons are lethal.'

'Her nature, Neem,' I repeat.

'Her body is built for killing,' he maintains, 'we can all see that, she's a killer.'

'We can only see her appearance. Her nature is who she is on the inside,' I insist.

'But her eyes, I mean they're not right, are they? The way she looks at you as if... as if...' He falters as he pictures Fitt's gaze resting on him when he was part of the crowd that stood before her and Flame. He frowns to himself as Nexus's love and affection help him to feel that which Fitt was broadcasting for all of them to know – that which at the time, his terror held away from him. That which he now can't deny.

'She's gentle and kind,' Neem says in a strangled voice, unable to believe his own words yet also unable to resist them being drawn from him by the combination of my horse's energy and his memory of Fitt's stare. 'She wants to help us, as many of us as possible, that's the reason she's here.' He shakes his head. 'But that can't be right.'

'Why not?' I ask him.

'Because she's a Woeful.'

'She's a Kindred. Why can't that be right?'

'She can't help us, she can't give us anything we need, anything we want, when she's so... so...'

'So...?'

'Different.' He says it as if it should explain everything when all it does is pierce Fitt's heart, just as she knew it would when her Awareness was nudged by our conversation about her.

Fitt will be okay and if she isn't, Flame will help her. My inbuilt need to see things through to their conclusion has reared its head and means that I can't let this go. I feel Nexus's warning and know I must tread more carefully than is my wont.

'You're afraid of Fitt because she's different from you,' I say to Neem as gently as I can. 'Nexus is different from you too, but you're accepting her help.'

*Yet humans resisted us too in the beginning,* Nexus informs me. *When the first of your kind took the first of mine to his village his friends were afraid and many carried murderous intent.*

*No!* The very thought that humans even considered attacking horses sends chills down my spine that are infinitesimally more intense than those caused by the cold.

*Centre yourself. Use the information I have given you.* Nexus is as calm and unmoved by her revelation to me as I am horrified, making it easy for me to follow her instruction.

Neem glares at me even as Nexus shuffles closer to him and rests her muzzle on his shoulder. 'Accepting help from a horse is not the same thing at all.'

I am pleased that I manage to keep my voice calm and devoid of judgement as I reply, 'According to Nexus, it's exactly the same, in fact she just told me that when Jonus and Mettle – they were the first bonded pair, you remember that, right?' When Neem nods with gritted teeth, I continue, 'Okay, well when Jonus took his horse back to his village after they bonded, his friends were terrified and lots of them wanted to kill Mettle. Thank goodness they realised their mistake and let Mettle guide them.'

Before I can say the rest of what I have in mind, Nexus intervenes as she so often does when she senses that my keenness to drive a point drive home will have the opposite effect. *Wait.*

I don't question her as I once would have. Now that I'm Aware, her interruption gives me the opportunity to pick up on that over which my personality would have trampled without her help; I instantly sense that Neem and his family need some time to digest what I've said if the rest of the words I have waiting are to have maximum effect.

My Bond-Partner doesn't need to tell me when the time is right to carry on. I am Aware of Fennel and Malek's need to be near Nexus, to have as great a sense of her as their intuition currently allows, even as they move to either side of her and begin stroking her neck and shoulder respectively.

I move closer too so that I can keep my voice as quiet as possible – so that I will disturb the family as little as possible as Nexus carries the energy of my words deep within those she is supporting.

'Being different is a blessing. Horses have helped us as much as they have because they're different from us; because they offer a different viewpoint and have different abilities from those we're capable of. The Kindred can help us progress even further by offering something else, something the horses have been guiding us towards all of this time. The horses and the Kindred are walking in step, you only have to see Fitt and Flame together to know that.'

'If they're walking in step, why can't it be the horses who help us? Why does it have to be Fitt?' Malek says.

I chuckle. 'The horses have had a hard enough time as it is, battering their way through to the minds of those they chose as their Bond-Partners, let alone trying to reach everyone else. Fitt is part human, so our minds recognise the touch of hers more easily. She can reach us all with as little effort as breathing. If you'll let her, she'll show you your connection to everything around you, including Nexus. Imagine knowing what my Bond-Partner wants you to know without having to wait for me to tell you.'

Malek's eyes shine in the lanternlight. 'That could happen? I'd be able to talk to her like you do?'

I smile at him. 'That will depend on how open you are, how

fully you embrace your Awareness and how keen you are to work through any blocks that restrict you, but it's definitely possible.'

'It would be amazing,' Fennel whispers to Nexus, gently pulling her fingers through my horse's mane. 'But how do I let Fitt help me when I can't even think of being near her without shaking?'

*The absence of fear is not a prerequisite for choosing to trust,* Nexus replies. *If it were then courage would not exist.*

When I relay my Bond-Partner's response to Fennel, she sags against Nexus, her words only just discernible to me. 'I want to be Aware of you, Nexus, to hear your thoughts for myself, but I've never been brave. What if I can't find the courage to trust Fitt?'

*It is not She Who Is Flame that you must trust. It is the voice of your soul. You were born with the ability to hear it. Listen to it when your fear would persuade you that anyone with a different appearance and life experience from yours is a threat. Listen to it and trust it for it alone knows why you are here and what is best for you.*

'The voice of my soul?' Fennel whispers on hearing my repetition of Nexus's counsel.

'Your intuition,' I murmur, not wanting to break the gentle, nurturing atmosphere that Nexus has created. I know it would be helpful to wait for Nexus's counsel to sink in, but she doesn't insist on it this time so I add, 'You don't have to try to not be afraid, you just have to choose to listen to your intuition despite being afraid. Fitt will do the rest.' *Sorry, Nexus, I couldn't help it.*

*I am aware of the compulsions retained by your personality. Were they detrimental to your balance then we would have addressed them. When they aid those drawn to you and me for the precise assistance our partnership can provide then it is appropriate they are expressed.*

I chuckle inwardly. *So what you mean is, no worries. I love you, Nexus.*

'Trust my intuition. I can do that,' Malek says. 'You can too, Dad, can't you? You've always told me to do it, right back from when I was tiny.'

Neem looks at me like a fox trapped by brambles. Then his shoulders lower and he grimaces. 'I guess I can do that, Son.'

Without knowing consciously that he's proving his point, he turns away from Nexus at his soul's urging, and steps out into the wind. I rub Nexus's forehead on my way past her and nod for Fennel and Malek to follow me as my horse heads back to her hayrack, her work done.

The three of us step out of the shelter into the rapidly falling darkness, Fennel holding up her lantern so that we can see our way. She stops at the sight of Neem at the fence separating their paddock from Shefali's. He is rubbing Flame's neck with both hands as she leans over the fence, her head over his shoulder, gently drawing him closer to her so that he can't help but feel her warmth. I am Aware of his surprise at what he feels; he thinks the heat blazing from my friend's Bond-Partner is purely physical. I can't wait for him to be Aware of everything else it is.

# SEVEN

## Fitt

*I* drain the last of the delicious stew that Shefali heated for us both, and lower to the floor the bowl that my hostess used her Awareness to select as a vessel I could easily use.

'That was delicious, thank you very much,' I say to the tiny female sitting happily opposite me, her legs crossed in front of her as if she always eats while sitting on the rug between her kitchen table and sink.

*You're welcome,* she replies. *I'm just glad I made a batch to freeze in the ice house, so it was sitting here ready and waiting; you were so hungry. If I say so myself, it was one of my better concoctions.* She swallows the last mouthful from her own bowl and her eyes glaze over as she immerses herself in the history of each ingredient that has just passed her lips, and then loses herself all over again in her Awareness of those who farmed them.

'I'm going to have to remind you to pull yourself back to your physical surroundings,' I tell her. On receiving no response from her, I add more loudly, 'Talking out loud helps with that.'

Shefali jumps and focuses on me. *But using mindspeak is so much more fun.*

I tilt my head to one side and raise my eyebrows.

'Oh, very well,' she says, 'I'll use my voice. Doesn't it sound loud in your head once you've used mindspeak though?'

'I've always been Aware so I've never thought about it, but judging by everyone else who's been through the process, you'll soon get used to it. You'll also get used to using exercises to centre yourself, like counting things or describing things you can see, hear, touch, smell or taste. Come to think of it, focusing on the ingredients in your stew was a fast track back into your Awareness – I suppose being a Baker means you're more used to using your intuition in combination with your sense of taste – so in your case, I think we'll stick with the other four senses.'

Shefali giggles. 'I love that you know I'm a Baker without me having to tell you, just as I love that I know all about you and your family without you having to tell me… oh, your mother misses you. And she's so worried about you.' Her eyes fill with tears as she senses my mother's feelings.

I can't allow myself to dwell on their emotions, or those of everyone else currently thinking about me, most of whom are much less well disposed towards me than are my mother and my new friend. I have to focus. 'Shefali, I want you to count the number of rocks in your kitchen walls. Come on, we'll do it together…' I wince suddenly and involuntarily as the conversation Aleks has been having with the family next door reaches the stage and depth of feeling I knew it would when it caught my attention.

Shefali gasps as her attention is drawn to that which now holds mine. Her words of outrage at Neem are lost to me even as their energy is held at bay by the warmth that immediately increases its presence in my mind. Shefali stops her tirade midstream as she senses that I am at peace once again. 'Wow. Flame just, I mean she just… wow.'

'Absolutely,' I say. 'Now, the rocks? We'll count starting from that corner.' I point to the corner above the sink.

Shefali flinches involuntarily and then flinches again as I quickly curl my finger so that its offending talon is hidden. She tears her eyes away from my hand and meets my eyes. I sense the emotional flinch that she manages to prevent from becoming physical as she links my slitted pupils to my clawed hands and remembers exactly who it is that she has taken into her home. She immediately takes refuge within her Awareness and relaxes as she finds me there. *I'm sorry, I shouldn't have reacted that way, it's just that… um, it's just that…*

'My appearance is taking some getting used to,' I say. 'I understand. Now, the rocks?' I count them with her, my need to do so having just increased tenfold.

As soon as I wake, my mind is full of Flame, just like it has been every morning since we bonded. We're both rested and comfortable, she lying in her shelter surrounded by pigs, I on a thick rug on the floor of Shefali's spare bedroom. Still mortified by her reaction to me following dinner yesterday, she almost cried in her desperation to get me to sleep on the large, sturdily made bed, but I steadfastly refused, explaining multiple times out loud as well as by showing her images of how we Kindred usually sleep, that I would be just as comfortable on the floor.

*Yet that was not why you refused,* Flame informs me pointedly.

My heart leaps at her thought – still so strange and yet so very welcome – then sinks a little at the knowledge that she is right. Humans do not shed hair from their entire bodies like cats and apes do. Like Kindred, as a result, do. I didn't want to face Shefali's horror at finding the amount of hair I am capable of leaving on her freshly laundered white sheets, or risk ripping the bedsheet in an attempt to clear it of hair myself.

*In refusing to embrace the physical differences between yourself and your host you render doing such an even greater challenge for her.*

I draw my knees into my stomach and curl up tightly around them in response to my horse's counsel. Her warmth is ever present but she doesn't increase it within my mind; I am Aware that while she will shield me from others when I need time and space in which to remember myself, she has no intention of shielding me from myself.

*You know how she reacted to me last night when I caught her by surprise,* I tell Flame. *How will flaunting my inhumanness make things easier for her? It will just make her more uncomfortable every time she can't help reacting that way and then feels she has to apologise.*

*And it will cause you pain that you believe you will have to find the strength to forgive. We already have that strength but when you make yourself smaller than you are in order to fit in then you will not feel strong.*

I've never resisted Flame's influence before – I've never wanted or needed to – but there is a part of me, very deep inside, that wants to resist it now. I'm relieved when a tap on the door provides a diversion from our conversation even as a sense of disquiet steals over me at the fact that I need one.

Shefali's voice is muffled by the thickness of the door. 'Fitt, breakfast will be ready shortly.'

I'm Aware that it is my favourite out of the options that humans favour to break their fasts – fried mushrooms and onions on toast with plenty of butter. I sense Shefali counting her footsteps as she hurries back downstairs to make sure that nothing is burning. I nod to myself. She is a very conscientious student.

I was drawn to her above the others in the crowd who were open to my help, because I knew she would be the most open of them – not only to her Awareness, but to me. Because in a way, she's like me. Unlike the other adults of her village, she has never been interested in having a mate or younglings, but has always preferred to spend her time expanding her knowledge of a range of different things. Where the concept of multiskilling confused and discomfited so many, for her it was welcome and she threw herself into practising every Skill from the moment she discovered it was possible. She has welcomed her Awareness like a long lost family member, and since little other than learning matters to her, she has few blocks to overcome in order to experience it at its fullest.

She connected with me so quickly, so fully, because like me, she is different. But even she finds aspects of me difficult. I can help with that.

Flame immediately repeats her warning to the contrary, but I put it to one side. I can be myself whilst also being an easier house guest for Shefali and a less imposing visitor to the village as a whole. I know I can. And I intend to start now.

I have to use two hands in order to turn the door knob whilst keeping my fingers curled inwards so that my talons aren't visible. It takes me a while but since I've never attempted it before, it stands to reason that it would.

'Fitt, shall I dish up?' Shefali calls, Aware of my difficulty opening the bedroom door and confused as to the reason.

*I'll be right there,* I reply, knowing that the construction of my throat won't allow me to call back loudly enough for her to hear, and desperate to distract her from both that fact and from sensing why my progress is so slow. *Since you're doing well at diverting yourself back to the physical from your Awareness, we'll work on you being able to focus on both at the same time now. Can you please ascertain how many villagers are awake whilst you are dishing up that amazing breakfast?*

I'm relieved that her attention is immediately diverted wholly towards her tasks, and she doesn't hear the door knob clunk loudly back to its original position when I lose my grasp of it. Happily, I managed to pull the heavy oak door open before it did so, and hurry out onto the landing.

When I reach the kitchen, I keep my eyes cast down and so sense rather than see Shefali smiling at me as she carries two plates of food to the table. She places mine atop it before sitting down on the rug adjacent to it with her own. I'm ravenous and mortified at having to lick my fangs so that saliva doesn't drip from them.

Shefali is still counting and doesn't notice, so I settle down opposite her with my plate.

'Ninety-four,' she tells me proudly. 'Dawn is late this time of year so those who work outside get a lie-in. Neem and Fennel are crop farmers so I was surprised to find them up already until I sensed why.' She smiles at me as I too sense her neighbours' keenness to achieve Awareness and the ability to communicate with the horses, tempered though it is by their wariness of me.

I give her the smallest of smiles in return so that my fangs can't make it into a snarl, then lower my eyes to my food so that she isn't faced with them for too long. Before she can sense the reason for my actions, I say, 'This is delicious, thank you. And well done, ninety-four is indeed the number who are awake. Now, can you eat one morsel of food at a time, each different in type from the one before it, while sensing how many sheep in all of the village's shelters are in lamb?'

'That will be easier,' she says. 'It was a bit weird moving

between the households in my Awareness, knowing things about everyone when they didn't know I was there.'

I refrain from telling her how strange that is to me when my kind have no need to keep anything secret or to dwell on anything we sense in each other that isn't relevant to our current task. I feel sure that the same will become true for her and her kind in time. Shefali discards everything she has just learnt in favour of her current task, proving me right.

I instantly knew the answer to the question I set her, but it will take her far longer to peruse her Awareness and find it. That means I have time to prepare for the arrival of Neem, Fennel, Malek and Tosca and her family, who are also now awake and eager to visit me.

Flame interrupts my thoughts. *Being yourself requires no preparation.*

*Being completely myself is counter-productive in this situation.* I brush away my concern that I'm also trying to convince myself. *I need to be enough of myself to be able to help, but I need to be sensitive to the fears of the people here so I don't make them worse.*

Flame doesn't reply but instead pushes at me with her warmth. I can feel her influence as easily and instantly as I've always been able to, but I'm Aware that there is part of me that is now closed to it – that wants to try things my way. Feeling strange at looking at things my way instead of ours, I begin once more to prepare for the morning's visitors.

The decisions I made during my preparation serve me well. I remain seated on Shefali's large, sturdy and very comfortable sofa when my visitors arrive and throughout their time with me. I lean forward, my arms on my knees so as to appear smaller, my fingers curled into my palms. I only glance at each of the humans very briefly, just long enough for them to feel once more the gentleness and willingness to help that I am very sure to broadcast their way. As soon as I feel them relax, I look away and immediately resonate my energy with the parts of theirs that I identified as being similar to mine before they entered the room. I don't see the looks on their faces as they feel their connection to me and then to Flame, but I am Aware of their feelings and have to focus hard on not scaring them with a smile at their gasps of delight.

I am also Aware of Aleks and Sonja's confusion. When it is replaced by sorrow in them both and an urgent pushing on my mind by Aleks, I focus my attention solely on those I am helping. When they are ready, I guide Neem and his family to Aleks's mind, and Tosca and her family to Sonja's, so that my friends' attention is then occupied with helping their charges to begin learning to centre themselves. While my plan works, it doesn't prevent my friends glancing frequently in my direction or battering at my mind whenever either of them have a few moments to spare.

I ignore them both other than to suggest it is time for them to take their charges home, and merely nod slowly, without making eye contact, when each of those I have taken to Awareness thanks me for my help. I am rewarded for all of my efforts by two happy families leaving Shefali's house without the slightest flinch having been necessary.

Once they have gone, I take a deep breath. As deep as I can manage, anyway; my chest feels tight and doesn't seem able to open fully, even when I slowly – so as to not cause Shefali any distress – sit up straight.

'Are you alright, Fitt?' my hostess asks me. 'You aren't

distressed, I can feel that, but I can also feel, and see, that you're different today.'

I have hidden my feelings and the reasons for my behaviour where she won't be able to find them. I'm careful to not hold eye contact with her as I say, 'I'm fine, thank you, just pacing myself as I have a busy day ahead of me. I won't get under your feet, I'll go out to Flame shortly so everyone else who comes can find me out there.'

Shefali probes at my mind, searching for a better explanation than she knows I have given. When she can't find one, I sense her hurt. 'I thought we were friends.'

I glance at her briefly. 'We are.' I almost smile at her so that she can see as well as feel the gratitude I send her way, but manage to stop myself. 'Thank you for having me, and for your help with everyone just now, I just need to prepare for my next visitor, that's all.'

The anguish that accompanies her stare almost pulls me out from behind the veneer I am just about holding together, but then I remember what happened yesterday evening and I hold firm.

'Right, well I'll just go and put the kettle on ready for whoever will arrive next then, shall I?' Shefali snaps. 'I know it's Farad, by the way. His intention is the strongest out of all of those who are preparing to come and see you, and he's just putting on his coat. Then it'll be Wit and Anjel, once they can stop arguing over whether it's going to start snowing again. And before you say anything, I'll recite nursery rhymes while I'm washing up this lot so I don't get too engrossed in my Awareness.' She picks up a tray of the mugs our visitors drained of tea before they left, and storms out of the room.

I hate myself for being the cause of her upset, but then steel myself as I realise that her anger is easier to bear than her fear.

# EIGHT

## Sonja

Once Tosca, her tall, broad-shouldered husband, Digh, and all of their children are occupied with exercises to ground them in their surroundings rather than actively perusing their Awareness, I turn my attention to Aleks, who has been waiting impatiently for me since setting the same exercises for his hosts. Though both families are focused on their tasks, we keep our thoughts small and focused so there is no chance they will pick up on them. Even so, Aleks makes me jump.

*WHAT ARE WE GOING TO DO? Fitt's not just blocking us out, she's doing it to Flame. I never thought she'd do this – when I found out what I did to her ancestors in that horrific previous incarnation of mine, when I hated myself for who I was, it was she who told me to love myself instead of being afraid. But here she is, hating herself and being afraid.*

*I know, it was hard to see her dumbing herself down like that. But if she won't let Flame help her through this, she won't let us and we shouldn't even try to push her about it. I think all we can do for the moment is focus our energy on helping our hosts be more confident in their Awareness than they currently are; it feels to me as though Fitt's reticence has rubbed off on them.*

*Agreed, I'm sensing the same thing,* Aleks replies. *We found it hard to tear ourselves away from our Awareness when we'd just found it, but my lot are almost relieved to do it. At least Fitt's decided to help everyone else to Awareness while in Flame's company, that should help.*

*I hope it does.*

It takes me some time to encourage my newly Aware host family away from the grounding exercises I set them and back to their Awareness, which, as Aleks observed, is the opposite of how I was when I was newly Aware and couldn't wait to explore everything I could suddenly know. I help them to move their attention from one thing to the next rather than dwelling on one place, person or subject due to their lack of confidence to explore, and the children's confidence soon builds. I switch to giving them exercises to ground themselves in the physical once more whilst continuing to encourage their parents to peruse their Awareness. I'm not sure which is more difficult – keeping six excited children calm and focused, or keeping calm myself in the face of doing such so that I can help Tosca and Digh. In the end, I use my horse as an incentive to achieve both.

'I know you've all been desperate to meet Bright, and you've done very well to wait this long,' I tell the children when they shout for what seems like the hundredth time that they've finished the exercise I set only minutes before. 'When you've counted the number of floorboards in each of the bedrooms – the eldest two of you each partnering with one of the youngest two to help them – we'll all go outside and see Bright before people start arriving for his counsel. Off you go and don't forget, I already know how many floorboards there are so I'll know if you cheat!'

The children all race for the door and thunder up the stairs, leaving Tosca, Digh and me in peace. 'Okay, now let's go and check in with Bright before we go and see him,' I say to my hosts, and am rewarded by both of them immediately and confidently darting straight to my horse. *Well done, that was perfect. You thought of the subject you wanted to investigate and then allowed your attention to go straight to him without holding back.*

My beautiful Bond-Partner rewards them by taking them with him for a mad canter around his paddock, bucking and squealing with delight when Nexus joins in two paddocks over. Tosca and Digh move their attention effortlessly to the mare and then on to Aleks, who welcomes them to join a conversation he is having with Neem and Fennel. Soon, all four of our hosts are enthusiastically sharing their experiences, and guiding one another to visit the subjects they've most enjoyed exploring.

I sense Aleks withdrawing from them alongside me, his satisfaction on a par with mine at their now rapidly increasing confidence. He picks up on my promise to the children and tells me, *Malek has already gone out to see Nexus, I'll see you outside in a bit.*

I stretch over the top of the smallest of Tosca's children for the door handle she can't yet reach.

'Kuli, let Sonja out of the door first,' her mother says, 'and all of you stay behind her once you're outside. There'll be no rushing down to Bright and absolutely no screaming. I know you're excited, but Bright will have a lot of people to see today and he doesn't need to start it by having to jump out of the paddock to escape a hoard of noisy children.' She winks at me, already Aware without me having to lead her to the fact, that there would be few circumstances in which Bright would feel the need to do any such thing, but also happy to have an enticement great enough to encourage a modicum of calm in her brood.

I step out into the snow for the third time this morning, glad that it is still not quite light; I have a little time yet before anyone will arrive to ask for Bright's counsel. I lift my knees up higher than normal in order to place my feet in the holes in the snow that Tosca, Digh and I have made on our trips to and from the sheep shelter. When Kuli immediately falls on her face behind me, her legs nowhere near long enough to do the same, I help Semmy lift her to her feet, brush the snow out of her face and before she can cry, say, 'Come on, I'll carry you so you can be the first to catch sight of Bright.'

Immediately, her face lights up and she stretches her arms up to me in anticipation of being lifted. I haul her out of the snow and onto my hip, then continue making my way to my horse.

'Are you alright there, Sonja? Hang on, I'll come and carry her, this snow's ridiculous,' Digh calls out from the back of our procession.

I'm delighted that his concern for me stems from his Awareness of my difficulty rather than his ability to see it over the heads of all of his family, and that as a result, he becomes Aware of Bright's intention to help me in the same instant that it is apparent to me. It is a further mark of how much his confidence has improved that he uses mindspeak to tell me, *Oh, okay, no need.*

I come to a slightly unsteady standstill, my already cold fingers gripping Kuli's thick over trousers in order to keep her in place on my hip. Semmy walks into me and then grabs hold of me to prevent me tipping forward onto my front. She grunts. 'Ow, Figal, step back, you're pushing me into Sonja.'

'Well, why have you stopped? Hurry up, I want to see... oooooohhhhhhhhhh, he's coming!'

The children stumble over one another and the snow in order to fan out behind me, all Aware that Bright is on his way but still mindful of their mother's instruction. I'm proud of them all.

Kuli stiffens against me and points a tiny gloved finger to where my horse is about to tear around the corner of the shelter into sight. When he does, his dark brown coat appears black against the snow through which he glides as if it weren't there. Balls of ice clink together in his thick, black forelock and mane as they lift and fall in time with his movement. His warm breath hangs in the air behind him before being dispersed by the cold breeze, and even in the dim light that has begun to bounce between the clouds and the snow, his eyes manage to shine brightly with his enthusiasm for life.

When he slides to a halt in front of me, there is silence. I glance back at Tosca and Digh, both of whom are now Aware of Bright's intention whilst also being grounded by their vigilance over their children. They are exactly where they need to be. They both smile and nod their agreement to my unasked question, as, frantically, does Kuli. Her little arms reach for my horse, and he moves closer. I lean against him as I hoist the little girl onto his back, savouring his warmth and his strength, knowing that he won't move until I've regained my balance.

*HOLD!* Digh tells the rest of his children, Aware that the sight of Kuli atop Bright almost made them forget themselves. *Wait for Sonja to tell you it's okay.*

I turn to them all with a grin. 'It's okay.'

I've always enjoyed visiting villages and witnessing people's reactions to Bright; I've always felt – though it matters not at all to him – that he so deserves the avalanche of love and respect that is always afforded him. But this is the first village aside from Rockwood that I've visited since being Aware; it is the first that Bright and I have visited in our capacity as Bond-Partners available not just to provide counsel but to mentor in the use of Awareness, and these are the first people for whom we've done that. I'm fascinated.

Kuli is the youngest and most excitable of the six children before me, but she is also the most open to her Awareness. She is currently the calmest of them all as she sits astride my horse, absorbing everything he is as if it's something she's done every day of her short life so far.

Semmy and Grant, being the eldest two children, are generally the calmest but the most prone to sibling rivalry, which is proving to be a block to them having as much access to their Awareness as does their youngest sister. They're Aware enough, though, to know that she has connected with Bright at a greater depth than they are managing and as a result, their emotions are the most volatile of the family. They have a hold on each other's cloaks, both of them trying to hold the other back so that they can reach Bright first.

The middling three children are Aware to differing degrees, but they don't follow the pattern set by their siblings of being less Aware with increasing age; Figal, the second youngest, has the most blocks in his way to full Awareness. He had a difficult incarnation last time around, I realise suddenly, then immediately bury that information before any of those around me pick up on it.

*You are wise to be mindful of how much any one mind can process at a time,* Bright informs me. He is a rock of serenity at the centre of a flurry of small hands all wanting to touch him, to rub his coat, to add a physical experience of him to the mental one they are having of him as they explore him in their Awareness.

Despite their differing blocks and abilities, one by one, the children reach the same calm, blissful state as Kuli. They sense the watchfulness of their parents and me, and all turn to look calmly at us, six young humans behaving and bearing the expressions of those who are anything but young.

*They won't always be like this, I'm afraid,* I tell the children's parents, careful to narrow my thought so that only they receive it. *Bright is helping them. You can always remind them to check in with him though. Wherever he is, whatever he's doing, he'll be available to them as he is now.*

Tosca and Digh are too awestruck and emotional to do anything but drink in the sight of their children clustered around my handsome stallion with his impossibly vibrant eyes.

'There's room for another one of you up there,' I say to the children, nodding at where Kuli sits happily picking ice balls out of Bright's mane. 'Who does Bright think it should be?'

Figal flushes red as his siblings all look at him, sensing the intense flares of jealousy in the four standing in the snow beside him. His bottom lip begins to wobble and his siblings sense his distress as if it is their own. Their jealousy immediately subsides, giving them the space to sense that Bright's choice arises from necessity rather than preference; Figal is the one who will benefit the most from a closer physical connection with my Bond-Partner.

Grant picks up his younger brother by the waist and lifts him to sit behind Kuli. There is compassion in his eyes as he looks up at Figal, and his hand rests upon the smaller boy's leg for longer than it takes Figal to find his balance and put his arms around his little sister's waist.

The interplay between the children is beautiful to watch. They are like birds flying and swooping together as a flock, their direction changing constantly and at speed as they respond to one another and their surroundings – in this case the all-knowing energy that is Bright – and their cohesion only strengthening as a result.

This won't do, I think to myself as I wipe a tear from my cheek before it can freeze. Tosca takes hold of my hand and squeezes it. *Thank you for being here with us, for staying here with Bright. And for bringing Fitt to Bigwood. Being Aware is everything you said it would be and more. What can I do to help you all with your task here?*

*What can WE do to help?* Digh adds as my horse turns slowly back towards his shelter, careful not to dislodge either of the children on his back or the two seemingly glued to both of his sides. The hands of the four older children remain buried in his fur as they walk with him back the way he came. The three of us follow.

*These are the villagers who will visit Fitt today of their own volition.* I bring to the forefront of my mind all of those who I sensed were open to receiving Fitt's broadcast of herself yesterday afternoon. *It would help us greatly if you could encourage as many of your friends as possible to visit her too.*

*What if they're too scared?* Digh asks.

*You could suggest that they come and ask for counsel from Bright or Nexus instead?*

*And if they won't?* Tosca asks me. *What if they're determined to avoid any attempt to help them be Aware?*

*Once there are enough of you who are Aware, we hope that, as a village, you'll agree to some of the Kindred coming to live here among you. Constant exposure to them over a period of time will increase the chance of those who are closed to their influence at first, gradually opening to it, and eventually allowing those Kindred to help them to Awareness.*

Their shock almost knocks me off my feet, and I'm glad Bright still has the children under his influence so that they are unaffected. I stumble and almost fall in the snow despite Bright having cleared a much easier path before us. Digh grabs my arm and Tosca, still holding my hand, lifts it up high while I find my feet.

*Sorry, but you want Kindred to LIVE here?* Digh asks, his attention flying involuntarily through his Awareness to the only Kindred he has met, its momentum then carrying him on to her parents. He relaxes as Lacemore and Ashwell welcome his clumsy intrusion, then relaxes further as they invite him and his wife to know all about them and their life with their daughter before she chose to be friends with us. The two Kindred don't try to hide their current concern for Fitt, and as parents themselves, my hosts identify with their anxiety. Their hearts go out to Lacemore and Ashwell… and then to Fitt herself.

We round the far end of the shelter beyond which Bright – still engulfed in children – has come to a halt at the paddock fence, and catch sight of Fitt brushing Flame's tail. Digh and Tosca both gasp.

*Why didn't we pick up on it before?* Tosca asks. *When she helped us to Awareness, she was the first one we sensed.*

*She allowed you to know the parts of herself she wasn't hiding from you,* I reply. *Now you've seen her through her parents' eyes, you can sense what's missing.*

Digh instinctively reaches out to Grant and hugs him. *No wonder her parents are worried about her. What do we do?*

*We give her as much love and support as we can and we trust her to find her way through it with Flame's help,* I tell him.

Tosca nods. *I keep forgetting she's Horse-Bonded. Do you know, it never occurred to me that you all might have problems too, you Horse-Bonded are always so calm and self-assured.*

I chuckle. *That's because when we're visiting the villages, we're usually helping all of you to deal with your problems rather than addressing our own.* Grateful that Fitt is intent on unravelling a particularly stubborn knot in Flame's mane, I add, *It just so happens that in this case, one has resulted in the other. In trying so hard to help you all, Fitt has strayed a long way from her centre.* I sense Tosca and Digh feeling their way around my thoughts on the subject.

'It's our fault,' Tosca whispers, guilt emanating from her with such force that it rouses her children from their perusal of Bright's life as a foal. All six turn to her.

I emit a subtle, almost imperceptible flow of light towards her, interrupting her emotion so that she turns her Awareness back to me and her children turn theirs back to Bright.

'Fault doesn't exist, not really. Fitt taught me that,' I say quietly. 'She doesn't hold any of you accountable for how she's feeling, you can sense that for yourself. She's in this situation for a reason, and at some point, that reason will become clear to her. In the meantime, we look out for her and help her as much as she'll let us, while continually putting what we know to one side so we don't contribute to making it bigger.'

Digh whistles to himself. 'Wow. Awareness is a double-edged sword, isn't it?'

I chuckle. 'It does seem like that to begin with.'

# NINE

## Aleks

$\mathcal{I}$ finish chipping ice out of Nexus's hoof and rub goose fat into her sole and frog to try to prevent more from lodging there. I stand up and pass Malek the hoof pick and jar of fat. 'There you go. Bend down by whichever foot you want to work on and when she lifts it for you, clean it out and treat it like I've just shown you. Keep your attention on your task, but notice what you sense in your Awareness at the same time without getting distracted by it. Balance what you can sense with what you're doing.'

Malek nods and bends down by Nexus's left hind foot. I feel the smile that lights up his face when Nexus lifts her foot and places it into his waiting hand. As soon as I'm happy that he's both strong enough to lever out the compacted ice, and disciplined enough to follow my instructions, I relax my guard over him and begin to brush my horse's tail. I notice that Fitt is doing the same for Flame. Tempting as it is to brush our horses' bodies with the long even strokes that provide them with pleasure, and us with a meditative sanctuary from our thoughts, we both know that doing so in winter would only deprive them of the oils their coats need to remain waterproof and warm. Brushing their tails is almost as relaxing, but not enough for Fitt to let go of the persona she thinks she needs to enact, or for me to get over the shock of seeing her almost as hunched as when I first met her.

Sonja and I, and now Tosca and Digh, judging by the conversation they're having, know that Fitt is protecting herself. Sonja and I came with Fitt on this mission to help her and I thought we had, but it turns out that we just helped her over the first hurdle and then left her floundering at the second. I sense Flame's warmth flowing through Fitt, inviting her to drop her guard, and I draw back, not wanting to add any pressure to Flame's gentle encouragement. But then I realise, to my chagrin, that it isn't an issue because Fitt isn't Aware of my scrutiny.

I can't prevent my eyes widening into the space rapidly vacated by my eyebrows. Of all the Horse-Bonded, Fitt has always been the most at ease with her Awareness, and by far the most accomplished. After she achieved perfect balance with Flame, her Awareness was unfettered. Absolute. It isn't now. Less than a day after arriving in a village of hostile humans, Fitt has formed a self-protective block to her Awareness.

My shock at the realisation draws Sonja's attention. I take a breath and quickly move past my discomfort before it attracts the attention of those less attuned to me than is my partner. Needless to say, neither her astonishment nor mine escape the notice of my horse, who informs me, *Balance can be precarious no matter how perfect. Perfection is no measure of strength but merely a point of reference to which to return.*

I frown. *Ummm, I guess that makes sense. The balance I find myself in when I'm riding you doesn't feel precarious though, I always feel strong, as if whatever you do, I'll be able to respond straight away and keep us both where we need to be.*

*Your strength arises as a result of imperfection having been fully explored and negotiated. You have returned to balance from every conceivable direction.*

I sense Sonja's amusement matching my own. *Thanks, Nexus, It's good to know I'm an example of how strong a person can be once they've messed up in every way possible. Fitt's already strong though. She aced her Findself despite finding it so tough, and not only that, she had the guts to go against her community and forgive the people of The Old for what they did to her ancestors. I'm only like I am now because she helped me so much.*

*That is why it is appropriate that you are one of those here to help her now,* Nexus informs me, bracing her leg so that Malek can use his hold on her foot to prevent himself flying after the chunk of ice he has just liberated from it. *Energy will always seek to find balance and it always does eventually.*

I begin to brush Nexus's mane while allowing her thought to settle within me. As it does, I become Aware of something else, something very subtle, almost insubstantial, that is pulling at me gently and, I realise all of a sudden, has been for some time. I acted upon it without consciously recognising that was what I was doing when I offered to accompany Fitt on her mission, and I now know it for exactly what it is; the thread that links the two of us will continue to hold us together until the energy between us has rebalanced.

I glance across to where Fitt continues to brush Flame's tail though it has long been free of tangles, and nod slowly to myself. I sense Sonja doing the same whilst distributing Bright's grooming kit to the four children jumping around her with their hands in the air.

*There still isn't much you can do for Fitt until she'll let you though,* Sonja observes. *We have to leave it to Flame to help her get to that point, don't we, and just support her the best we can in the meantime.*

*We can help Flame to help her,* I reply. *Fancy going for a ride at lunchtime? The horses will have been standing around for a while by then, judging by the queues building over there.* I take her attention with mine to where villagers have begun to wait quietly in line by each of the three paddock gates. I wave to Neem to signal that Nexus and I are ready, and he opens the gate to admit our first visitor of the day just as Shefali enters her own paddock with a man walking with his body turned slightly back towards the gate, as if he will turn and run at any moment.

*Great idea, I think we'll all be ready for a break by then. Have a good morning, Aleks.* I sense Sonja's concern as she too watches Shefali stride confidently towards Fitt and Flame while the man shuffles uncertainly through the snow behind her.

*Fitt needs to go through this as much as I needed to put myself through everything I did,* I remind her and sense her relax. *Have a good morning.*

We both watch as Fitt suddenly notices that she and Flame are no longer alone in the paddock. We sense her unease as she takes in the sight of the queueing villagers, and her Awareness of the feelings of most of them towards her. She defies her desire to race towards the privacy of Flame's shelter, instead moving slowly, carefully, so as not to cause alarm to her onlookers. She disappears inside and Flame soon follows suit.

'I suppose I'd better go,' Malek says, stroking Nexus's nose with the back of his forefinger. 'The wind's picking up again so you'll be better off seeing everyone in the shelter. Or I could pass on Nexus's advice to them while you help the ones Fitt will take to Awareness? I could, you know.'

I grin at him. 'I know you could. The trouble is, they won't ask Nexus what they really want to if you're here. You're a fellow villager of Bigwood but I'm just me.'

He kicks at the snow and sighs.

'You could encourage your friends and their families to come and see Fitt though. Can you help Nexus and me out that way instead?'

'I suppose so.'

'Good lad. Run along then, we'll see you later.'

The morning passes in a flash. Nexus and I receive a continuous flow of visitors, all of whom go away far more open to visiting the neighbouring paddock in the coming days. In addition to passing on Nexus's counsel to them, occasionally with an addition of my own in order to expedite their understanding and departure, I flit between those Fitt guides to me to be coached in balancing their newly acquired Awareness with their grasp on normal life.

Neem and Fennel refrain from going to work; Fennel so that she can work her way around her friends with the same aim as that with which Malek approaches his, and Neem in order to organise those waiting and departing – a few of whom immediately join the queue waiting to see Fitt – and so that he can be sure to bring me everything Nexus and I need as soon as he is Aware that we need it. As a result, I am heavily wrapped against the cold and well supplied with hot drinks and snacks. Nexus has the ice broken every half hour on the water trough she shares with the donkeys, and her dung removed while it is still steaming.

Unused to being so closely monitored and attended, or so fully occupied with all those needing the various kinds of assistance I can now provide, I am as keen as I sense are both Sonja and Fitt for a little peace and quiet at the end of the morning.

*But I've made you some soup,* Neem replies when I let him know that Nexus and I will be departing for a short while.

*Thank you, I'll look forward to it on my return, but Nexus needs to stretch her legs with Flame and Bright. We'll be back before you know it, if you could let those who are waiting know.*

It pleases me that Neem uses my thought as a conduit to sensing that my need to ride out surpasses purely a desire to accompany my horse while she exercises, yet resists probing any deeper in favour of answering someone who has just called out to him from the queue. When he's done with them, he merely replies, *Fair enough, I'll hold the fort here and see you when I see you.*

*I appreciate it.*

I turn my attention to Fitt. Doing so would normally be enough for her to register my intention to communicate with her, but she is oblivious and continues instead to focus upon shutting a significant part of herself away. I am Aware that she is sitting atop a small hay bale with her elbows on her knees, as she has all morning in order to give the appearance of being as small and unthreatening as possible to those who plucked up the courage to approach her. She is stiff and aching as a result, and cold, which is something I've never known her to be before. Flame stands as close to her as possible in order to give Fitt both her body heat and support, but neither are enough to keep my friend comfortable. Bowls of soup and tea brought out by Shefali lay untouched by the bale of hay since Fitt hasn't risked being seen drinking from one in the Kindred way by any of her visitors.

I take a deep breath as if I am going to shout, because I intend to do the mental equivalent of exactly that. I focus upon Fitt's mind as I announce with as much force as I can, *Nexus is all for going over the back fence to stretch her legs in the pasture beyond, and by all accounts, Bright and Flame are up for joining her. Come on, let's go!* I'm careful to accompany my thought with

a sense that it isn't in question whether or not Fitt and Flame will
come with us.

*I'm in,* Sonja agrees. *The snow's deeper by the fence so it'll be
easier for the horses to jump it without our weight. We'll join them
on the other side, shall we?*

Fitt's response is muted, as if she's calling out from far away. *I
think I'll wait here.*

*No way,* I tell her, *you've been as hard at it all morning as
Sonja and I have. We all need some time out if we're to be as
helpful to the people who'll come to see us this afternoon as we
were to the ones this morning. Come on, if I'm Aware how keen
Flame is, her enthusiasm must be overwhelming you.*

Nexus helps me out by whinnying so that Flame responds in
kind. I am almost deafened by my horse's voice as it bounces
between the walls of the shelter, but I smile even as I cover my
ears. My beautiful mare has been her usual patient, gentle, kind
self in the face of all of those who have cried, ranted, paced, even
raged at her counsel to listen to their inner voices instead of the
loud physical ones that would convince them of the danger posed
by Fitt. She has comforted, soothed and very gently cajoled each
and every one of them to the conclusion that they must follow
their own guidance as much as hers, and visit our Kindred friend.
It is music to my ears to now hear her expressing her power and
strength, her beauty and spirit as she calls to the other horses to
rise to her challenge.

My beautiful grey mare turns her head in my direction, her
long white eyelashes angled upwards as her eyes widen. Her
nostrils flare and her ears swivel in all directions as she senses
Bright and Flame preparing to move.

We both sense Bright bursting from his shelter into the
sunshine that has just broken through the clouds. Nexus quivers as
she both senses and listens to the powerful stallion ploughing his

way through the snow two paddocks away. Knowing that it will take all of us as well as Flame to pull Fitt out into the open, she thunders out of the shelter with me in hot pursuit, both of us revelling in the sun's rays even as they blind us by rebounding off every snowflake they meet so that we can only feel, rather than see, our way.

We are with Bright as he uses the deeper snow to aid his sudden decrease in speed in front of the fence. He almost sits down before jumping with elegance and precision over the fence, his balance never wavering as he lands on the other side and turns to wait for Sonja. His confidence in himself touches us all.

Nexus reaches the fence next and, still blinded by the dazzling snow, I feel rather than see her doing exactly as did Bright. Her body isn't as compact as the stallion's – she is taller and longer through her back – so she has to work much harder to gather her slender body together when the deep snow would tease her long hind legs away from underneath her. I'm never in any doubt that she'll balance herself, and revel in her strength as she sails gracefully over the fence and lands beside Bright as if the fence were merely an obstacle she had to step over.

Flame is a mass of barely contained energy as she dances on the spot by Fitt, all of her senses focused on Bright and Nexus so that Fitt can't help but be drawn to them too, then to Sonja and me as we gambol through the snow after our horses. The two of us laugh as we trip and stumble, our eyes almost shut so as to protect them from the brightness, loving the fact that we need nothing other than our Awareness of our horses to guide us to where they stand waiting for us.

*COME ON!* I shout to Fitt in my mind, attaching my Awareness of Flame's desperation to my thought so that she is bombarded with it from all sides.

When Flame erupts from her shelter at blistering speed, snow flying to all sides in clouds as if it were the finest of powders, Fitt can't help but follow despite her worry about scaring those who are watching. Her concern recedes as she realises that not only are they all mesmerised by the snow explosions being created by her Bond-Partner, but the resulting clouds are hiding her exit from the shelter.

Flame's power and confidence draw Fitt onward, even if she does skulk along the fence line so that she continues to be hidden from the crowd by the shelter until she is almost at the fence, by which time Flame stands waiting with Nexus and Bright. All three horses are breathing hard as a result of their exertions, but all three are keen for us to mount and be away from Bigwood.

I let out a slow, silent breath of relief when Fitt climbs the fence far more slowly and carefully than she needs to, and tentatively mounts her horse.

TEN

Fitt

_I_ don't feel well. Not ill as such, just strange as I settle into place on Flame's back. Although that's just it, I suddenly realise – I'm not settling into place, because I can't find it. Even the thought of needing to find it is strange to me when I usually just mount and am exactly where I need to be, but right now I definitely feel all wrong.

*You know the reason,* Flame informs me. She has been quiet all morning, content to stand by my side and snooze, barely paying attention to those who only let me show them to Awareness as a result of her reassuring presence. She begins to move beneath me before I can form a response.

I feel as I did when I first sat on her back; precarious and unsure of myself but determined to stay in place. I clamp on to her sides with my legs and take hold of chunks of her mane. Even so, I'm almost unseated as Flame practically jumps her way through snow that has drifted across the pasture to accumulate against the fence. I hang on, hoping we will soon reach snow that is shallower.

Bright and Nexus move into position on either side of Flame, their movements far less awkward than hers, their riders sitting effortlessly, fluidly, easily absorbing their horses' movement like I normally can.

'Just relax, Fitt,' Sonja says softly, all trace of the hilarity that she and Aleks have been enjoying now absent. 'It's just us now; you and Flame, me and Bright, Aleks and Nexus. Just relax and be yourself.'

Her words shock me and I can't think why. Flame takes hold of them and carries them deep within me, refusing ever so gently to let me move past them. I want to cry as I haven't since I was a youngling. I sit up a little straighter on Flame's back and feel a little more comfortable there.

*Cry, Lacejoy.* My mother's use of the name she and my father gave me shocks me, but causes me to sit up a little more still.

*We've all got you. Cry,* my mother insists and I realise that she is not alone in reaching out to me. Father, Elder Hobday, Amarilla and Katonia are all with her. Bright moves close enough for Sonja to rest a hand on my leg and Nexus does the same so that Aleks can place his on my shoulder.

'Let it go, Fitt,' Aleks says. 'See it for what it is and let it go. All of it. I know you can. Flame knows you can. Let her help you.'

Flame lurches suddenly. Were it not for Bright and Nexus hemming us in between them, and Aleks and Sonja leaning into me, I would have been unseated. The wrongness of my body, the wrongness in myself, jars against the soft, loving energy of all those who know me so well. A tear rolls down my face as Flame almost unseats me again. I feel so alone, so detached from everything that used to feel comfortable, but I can't go back to being how I was. I can't be that big and scary if I am to do that which I know I need to do – that which I was born to do.

*You can.* Flame's thought drifts into my mind rather than arrives accompanied by her usual calm determination. *You should.* Her energy is weaker. She is weaker, I realise as she stumbles beneath me. I lurch forward and only the strength in my legs saves me from landing on her neck.

'You're unbalancing her, Fitt,' Sonja says gently. She squeezes my thigh with her fingers whilst easily sitting Bright's extravagant efforts to lean into Flame. 'It's ok, you can fix this.'

How can this be? I have perfect balance, as has Flame.

*Not at present,* my horse informs me. No judgement accompanies her thought, no concern, she merely states the fact as a mild observation. *You have created a persona within which you feel safer but it has only served to pull you from your centre.*

*But I was being pulled from my centre before.*

*By your desire to feel accepted and nothing more.* She stumbles again and my heart goes out to her... where I can't protect it. She immediately encloses it within her warmth and I begin to cry with a force that is as unfamiliar to me as the position in which I am sitting.

My friends and their horses remain supporting Flame and me until I am weak from crying – and yet stronger all of a sudden. I shift my position on Flame's back and am immediately able to help my horse to balance beneath me.

Bright and Nexus peel away from Flame. The snow is shallower now and the three horses begin to canter, the love of my horse carrying me as strongly as does her body. My family and friends remain with me, their sense of who I am to them strengthening my sense of myself until I have cried out everything that I am not. I am Lacejoy, daughter to Lacemore and Ashwell; I am Kindred and proud to walk tall; I am Fitt of the Horse-Bonded; I am Bond-Partner to Flame; I am the bringer of Awareness to the humans of The New.

*That is who you are to everyone else,* Flame observes. *Who are you to yourself?*

The answer comes easily to me now that I am back where I should be. *She Who Is Flame. I'm sorry I couldn't hold on to myself.*

*It is of no matter. We chose this situation because of the challenge it presents. Because of the learning and strength you will gain as a result. Because of what that strength will bring to those we will meet in the future. Now that you have found your way back to your centre you will find it easier to do the same from subsequent departures.*

*This isn't over.* My thought starts out as a question but is a statement by the time it is complete, my Awareness having returned to those awaiting me in Bigwood. Immediately, I want to curl over, to make myself smaller, to protect myself and them.

Flame jumps to the left and Nexus does the same in order to stay out of her way. While Aleks absorbs his horse's movement as if it were nothing, I am forced to clamp on with my right leg in order to stay on Flame's back. I make the adjustments needed in my body and mind, and Flame settles back into step with the rhythmic, powerful canter of the other two horses.

I lose myself in my horse and all we are. By the time the paddocks of Bigwood come back into view, we know that we won't be returning to them over the fence. The villagers who came to see us this morning were those who knew my intentions, who felt my desire to help them when my friends and I arrived at Bigwood yesterday. Those waiting to see me this afternoon were closed to my broadcast of myself yesterday. They are here at the urging of their friends or following counsel from Nexus and Bright, and they will not let me help them to Awareness if I cannot confirm the wisdom of their decision by showing them who I am first.

Nexus, Bright and Flame turn as one and head away from the fence, towards one end of the village. The three horses slow to a walk as we approach the compacted snow covering the cobblestones of Bigwood's main street, but they move with no less power and elegance. I look straight ahead so as not to alarm anyone with an unwelcome glance, but when the temptation arises to round my shoulders, I catch myself and manage to remain with Flame.

When we reach our hosts' cottages, Bright and Sonja peel away from us first. They leave without thought or comment but when a burst of light touches me, I turn to see Sonja looking back at me with a warm smile.

As Flame leaves the slippery street that she has been gliding over as if it were a sand track, another flow of light boosts me further. It is less intense than that which Sonja generated, but is accompanied by a sense – no, a very intentional reminder – of the thread that extends between Aleks and me. When I was first Aware of it, back when he and I first met, it drew me to him so that I was ready for when he needed me. Now it holds him to me and he would use it to remind me that we incarnated in this lifetime together in order to help one another – that while Flame is most of what I need, he is there for a large portion of the rest.

I look back to where Aleks and Nexus are waiting on the street, and smile as broadly as my fangs allow. He grins back while continuing to direct light in my direction. It is almost imperceptible to the eye but continues to carry the energy that I showed him, and of which he would serve as a reminder to me in return.

Two villagers stop to hold out their hands for Nexus to sniff, but instead gasp as they catch sight of what they perceive to be my snarl. I remember that I am not only here to help them to Awareness but to remind them to listen to their intuition instead of their fear as did their forefathers. Both my presence and theirs is as it needs to be and we will all benefit. I continue to smile as Aleks punches the air.

Flame carries me between Shefali's and Fennel's cottages as if my weight is no problem at all for her to bear, because it isn't now that all of the parts of our bodies are moving in harmony and supporting each other as they should. I hold firmly to who I am as we approach the back of the queue of humans waiting to see me, and glance at each of them in turn as Flame powers past them. I feel glad that they are only half as terrified after picking up my broadcast of myself, as they were before.

Shefali smiles up at me as she opens the paddock gate, Aware that she is looking at the version of me that she befriended yesterday.

*I'm so glad you're feeling better,* she tells me, then adds out loud, 'I knew you were on your way so I've left a hot meal for you in the shelter. I put it on top of the straw stack so the pigs can't reach it, but they shouldn't bother anyway, they're happy out here in the sun for now.' She nods over her shoulder to where her enormous black pigs are rooting around in the snow for the vegetables she has scattered.

Flame makes us both laugh by snorting at her shelter companions, who appear very different to her now that they are moving around and honking rather than buried deep in the straw bed as they have been since our arrival. A wave of fear and revulsion blasts into my back from the queue, and I stop laughing.

Shefali scowls at her friends as Flame stretches her neck up high in front of me, lifts her tail and snorts again. She takes a step back from the pigs as if she is scared of them – and I am Aware that she now is. Her body is rigid and her heart is thumping wildly. In contrast, Nexus and Bright calmly pass the pigs on either side of the paddock on their way to their own shelters, Sonja and Aleks each chatting with the villager who has left the front of their queue to accompany them. My friends and my horse are again highlighting my problem so that I can see it for what it is.

We Are Flame. I shift within myself and Flame gathers herself in response. We are powerful once more. Flame prances down to the shelter as if we are the only ones there, for in truth, we are. All of those waiting to see us are us and very soon, they will know it.

I dismount in the shelter and rub Flame down while she pulls hay from the makeshift hay rack in the corner. I appreciate it being full when it was almost empty before we left only a short time ago; Shefali is a most attentive and generous host, as are the families living either side of her who donated hay from stores intended to keep their sheep and donkeys through the winter.

*Everyone else in the village will make sure they have what they need if they run out before spring,* Shefali assures me, sensing my gratitude and concern. *I'll send your first visitor of the afternoon down once I know you've eaten,* she adds pointedly.

My stomach rumbles in response, alerting me to the fact that I am famished. I check the water barrel and am pleased to find that the ice has been recently broken. I hurry to the straw stack where a large bowl sits beside a huge cookpot of steaming stew. I fill the bowl, sensing the care Shefali took to browse her Awareness of me and select the ingredients she found to be my favourites. As I eat the stew, the love she put into preparing it seeps into me along with her hope that I would eat it and her concern that I would disregard it as I have everything else she has prepared for me. I finish the bowl, then refill and empty it several times until the cookpot is empty.

*Thank you.* My thought carries far more to Shefali than my gratitude for the meal.

*Thank you, Fitt. For everything.* My host is talented in the use of her Awareness, her reply conveying as much as mine and more, yet its components subtly entwined and delivered gently so that they almost feel as if they were mine to begin with – a far cry from the usual bombardment from someone newly Aware. Further, Shefali is interacting fully with those around her while doing it.

*Katonia...*

*On it,* my friend replies as if waiting for me to ask – which I'm now Aware she has been.

I curse myself for having shut myself away from everything that was going around me this morning, but Katonia pulls me away from my frustration. *You're back now and that's all that matters. I'll work with Shefali. She's easily confident enough to work with someone she hasn't met physically, and strong enough to help those coming to Awareness behind her once I've shown her how. That will lighten the load for Aleks and Sonja.*

Lighten the load? I sense that it is heavier than it should be and though Katonia tries to hide the reason for it, she isn't quick enough. My friends aren't just helping people to centre themselves, they're having to work hard to get them comfortable using their Awareness at all because of how I've been behaving.

*Fitt, it's okay, we all understand...*

*It's not okay,* I interrupt Katonia. *I need to do better. Much better. Thank you, my friend.*

*Have a good afternoon, Fitt.* She moves her attention to Shefali, who welcomes it as if the two of them are old friends, while also opening the gate for the first of those waiting to see me.

I decide to continue sitting on a hay bale as I did all morning, but when a teenage youngling enters the field shelter, I raise my eyes to meet hers and smile. Having identified the aspects of her that we have in common while she was nervously picking her way across the compacted snow to me, my energy is already resonating with hers. When she catches sight of me, our connection solidifies and pulls her away from her hesitation at my strangeness.

I bury the splinter of hurt that I can't seem to avoid feeling, and remain seated as the youngling grasps hold of the doorframe to steady herself at the touch of my mind on hers. She has many blocks in place to experiencing full Awareness, but not so many as to block her from knowing me. I sense her astonishment as she reconciles what she now knows with what she previously thought, and guide her to Flame, whose warmth delights her. She walks slowly towards my mare, altering the angle of her approach and the language of her body in line with what she senses will be most acceptable to Flame. She holds out her hand and when Flame has sniffed it, gently strokes her cheek.

When she is ready, I guide her mind to Sonja's, sensing that she alone of my friends is free to engage with the youngling. I take my attention swiftly to the next in line to see me so that I can't focus on that which I would prefer not to. I am almost quick enough. I almost manage to ignore the fact that my shoulders are a little hunched once more, but not quite.

By the time the afternoon has passed, sixteen more villagers are Aware to varying extents. I should be happy but I'm not. None of the sixteen are having trouble remaining cognisant of their physical lives and surroundings, and not because they are exceptionally good at the exercises Aleks and Sonja have set them to ensure it, but because like all of the others before them except Shefali, they aren't as confident in their Awareness as they should be.

The youngling I saw first is the most confident despite having more blocks than those who came after her. The adult male I saw last is by far the least confident despite having only a few blocks, because by the time he visited me, the fragments of hurt and self-doubt I felt as a result of the reactions of all those before him had accumulated and become too much of me. I was unable to smile or meet his eyes, and when I searched for aspects of ourselves that we shared, I found that it was lack of confidence and fear that bound us most strongly. Though they allowed us to resonate, and him to awaken to our connection, and though I was immediately able to guide him to Flame so that he could experience the beauty of his newly awakened ability, he couldn't help but be affected by how he arrived at it. His sorrow for me didn't help either of us, and it won't help to shorten the day for Aleks or Sonja, who will need to visit all of the newly Aware this evening in order to give them the confidence to then be able to work with Shefali.

I can't do this, I'm letting everyone down.

*You need merely find your way back to the place whence you departed,* Flame reminds me. *It will be easier this time.*

I remember our ride at lunchtime. *I suppose. Doing so won't change the fact that I can't seem to stay there though – that I'm being as much a hindrance as a help to the people here.*

*It will allow you to continue your learning. You know this truth. You have already imparted it to others. Your current learning will ensure that the truth you know from one angle becomes unassailable from each and every other.*

Something begins to lighten within me. I do know the truth. I used it to forgive all that was done to my ancestors.

*So now I need to forgive myself?*

*You should apply the same truth to every situation and from every angle,* Flame repeats patiently. *Use each instance of straying from your centre to fully examine the energy involved in your return.*

*You don't want me to do it by riding you this time.* I'm not asking her, for I know. By phrasing her communication in order to reach me when my current difficulties would hold her mere influence at bay, she has influenced me to phrase my thoughts to myself – to make them more obvious to me, more difficult to ignore. Which is intentional on her part, I realise. *You don't want me to find my centre by riding you because I have to forgive my way back to it.*

I get to my feet and stretch. My shoulders lift and straighten as I stand tall, my pain at the reactions I elicited from my visitors falling away from me as easily as my guilt at causing extra work for Aleks and Sonja, as I embrace the truth. Everything is happening as it is meant to.

Love for my horse, my partner, my teacher, floods through me along with the understanding she has brought. I may be as animal as she in many ways, but it is the part of me that is human that she coaches and to which she constantly adapts herself in order to help me.

I can do this.

ELEVEN

## Sonja

*B*y the time I got to bed last night, I was too tired even to undress. I have woken this morning to what sounds like hundreds of people racing up and down the stairs, along the hallway, in and out of the bedrooms and bathroom, but is in fact, I realise as I come fully to, just six very energetic children. Yet other than their footfalls, they are making no sound; there is none of the yelling, shrieking, arguing or scolding that met my arrival the day before yesterday – not out loud, anyway.

*Ow, Walter, you trod on my foot!* Semmy complains.

*Did not, it was Kuli.*

*I think I can tell the difference between her little feet and your big ones.*

*Touch the biggest piece of wood in each and every room in the house except Sonja's, five times,* Digh reminds his brood.

*Oh Daaaaaaaaad, can't we just go and see Bright instead?* Figal pleads while tagging the headboard of his parents' bed.

*Bright won't always be here,* Digh replies. *You need to get used to being with him in your mind if you're feeling unsteady, and that means being able to find him while you're also doing whatever you're supposed to be doing physically. Semmy and Walter, while you're standing there arguing, Kuli has raced ahead of you both.*

There is an immediate increase in the pounding of feet. I grin wearily as I sit up and rub my eyes. When I embarked on this trip with Fitt, I expected a lot of things but I had no idea how rewarding it would be to witness people embracing the new way of life she has instigated.

I also didn't foresee that I would need to leave Fitt to struggle with minimal intervention, or how exhausting it would be to take up the slack for her. She did much better yesterday afternoon than in the morning, but where Aleks and I had hoped to give the newly Aware villagers exercises to ground themselves and then check on them regularly to make sure they were doing them, none of them returned to their Awareness at all until we visited them physically, one by one, in the evening and coached them in the same way we did with our host families.

We got there with them all, even to the point that we could guide them to Shefali's mind so that she can check in with them today, but soon there will be too many for her to handle. My hope is that they will be confident enough by the end of today that she can introduce them to the mind of a stranger – Katonia or maybe Jack – in order to lighten her load. What we really need is more Horse-Bonded here to help us.

*It's in hand, Sonn, I just checked,* Aleks informs me. *Welcome back to the land of the living, by the way. Are you getting up any time soon?*

*I am up.*

*Sitting on the bed in yesterday's clothes with your eyes only half open doesn't count.*

Rowena intervenes before I can form a retort. *Give it a rest,*

*Aleks, we can't all be pinging out of our skins all the time like you and Justin. Like I just told him, Sonja, Marvel and I have arrived at The Gathering with Holly and Vic. Between us and Quinta, we'll soon have everyone organised to travel to the villages you leave in your wake, starting with Bigwood.*

*You mean you'll have everyone organised before the rest of us have had a chance to draw breath.* Marvel's teasing and affection for his partner lighten a thought that is otherwise heavy with fatigue.

*She absolutely means that and thank the light she does,* Aleks enthuses.

*We'll have the first two on their way to you this morning,* Rowena continues as if only she and I are party to the conversation.

*You're shattered, you've travelled practically non-stop to get there,* I reply, concerned for all four of my friends as I sense them staggering around in one of the larger field shelters, making sure their horses have everything they need.

*The weather was only getting worse and it was easier to carry on than listen to Marvel moaning about it,* Rowena tells us to the tired amusement of the other three.

*I doubt I have to convince you that it was Rowena wanting to get here as soon as possible so that the organising couldn't begin without her,* Marvel retorts.

*Well, we couldn't leave it to Quinta,* Rowena fires back. *She's had enough on her plate. It's thanks to her that we have Horse-Bonded here who are even ready to coach people when they've only just come to Awareness themselves.*

*Yet you've been happy to leave her to it up until now. Is it at all possible that you just like to be where the action is?* Marvel asks her.

I sense Vickery and Holly sending their love to Aleks and me as they slip out of the shelter and head for the buildings. I return their love along with a burst of strength to help them slide their way along the path under the weight of their saddles and saddlebags. I am relieved to sense Quinta, Mason and three others on their way to meet and help the two of them, Rowena and Marvel, whose fatigue is in no way affecting their ability to spar.

*I could say the same about you,* Rowena retorts, *you're always right there with me and...*

Aleks interrupts her. *Well anyway, thanks, guys, for getting there so quickly. Oh, and also for waking Sonja up properly, it looks like she might be ready to face the day after all. There's nothing like the entertainment that only Marvel and Rowena can provide to make the rest of the day seem less of a challenge, is there, Sonn?*

I chuckle as I step onto the landing, immediately hugging the wall to avoid being run headlong into by Grant. *Nothing at all. Thanks, all of you, I'm definitely up and running now. Ro, Marv, please get some rest before you get stuck in?*

*They absolutely will, I'll see to it,* Quinta tells me firmly. *And don't even think of arguing with me, Rowena, you know how much organising I've had to do these past weeks – sorting you out won't even come close in terms of difficulty. Mason and Turi are on their way to get your stuff, and there are baths being run for you all as we speak, so prop yourselves up on each other and make your way to the buildings.*

*What's funny?* Semmy catches my smile as I pass her, and latches onto the conversation of which I'm a part.

I put a suggestion of a block in between it and her. *Do you remember the exercise we did on moving past things that you can sense but which don't involve you?* I ask her.

She nods, flushes red and immediately withdraws her probing. She senses my approval and smiles sheepishly before racing into the bathroom ahead of me, touching the bath panel and racing back out.

'Does anyone else need to tag anything in the bathroom before I have a bath?' I yell towards the continuing thunder of footsteps.

*Me!*

*Me!*

*Me!*

*Me!*

*Me!*

I wait for all five children to run in and out of the bathroom, then hurry in and shut the door.

*Sorry, Sonja.* Tosca's thought rings with embarrassment. *We didn't think the ramifications of this particular exercise through. We'll get better at it as the days go by.*

*You're already doing brilliantly, their task has them well grounded.*

Relief precedes her thought. *Breakfast is ready when you are. I've made loads because judging by yesterday, you're going to need it.*

Tosca wasn't wrong; the day passes with Aleks and me every bit as busy as we were yesterday. The days that follow are even busier. They all start with the two of us eating our breakfasts outside in the cold with Fitt so as to enjoy some time with one another and our horses before our first visitors arrive. We spend the mornings working through our respective queues and then have another brief reprieve at lunchtime before getting back to it for the afternoon, eating a hurried dinner and then setting back out to visit in person all of those who visited Fitt during the day.

While we have always been required to see one person after

another during the first few days of visits to villages, the queues usually die down after that, leaving us a few easier days before moving on to the next village. Five days after our arrival in Bigwood, the queues aren't showing any signs of dying down. Our hosts have done an excellent job persuading those of their friends who were too scared to visit Fitt straight away, to come and see us, and our horses have in turn done an excellent job directing them to listen to their intuition and go to see Fitt.

As more villagers realise their connection to each other and everything around them, they in turn use what they know to persuade even more of the residents of Bigwood to follow suit.

As a result, our days continue to be filled with passing on our horses' counsel, and our evenings with visiting those needing our physical presence to give them the confidence to explore their Awareness. Those whose homes we visit now need less of our help, less of our time, than those we visited on day two due to Fitt very slowly finding the confidence to be more herself with each passing day, but they do still need our time.

We have been in Bigwood for seven days by the time Elinora and Quinta ride into the village on Resolute and Spider, the stocky black stallion with his luxuriant mane walking step for step with the lighter, more athletic brown one. Aleks and I wave to our friends as the villagers of Bigwood stream from their homes to welcome them.

*About flaming time,* Aleks observes. *Sonn and I were just on our way to do our evening visits but I'm thinking that since you've been languishing in Rockwood, you'll be good to take over?*

Elinora sticks her tongue out at him as she slides down from Resolute's back.

Quinta replies, *I'd hardly call being waylaid by Amarilla's mother "languishing" but yes, we can absolutely take over once we've got the horses settled in.*

I ease my way through the crowd until I'm standing in front of the petite Horse-Bonded whose hair, still tied back in the tail she has always favoured, is significantly greyer than when I last saw her. 'You'll do no such thing,' I say and hug her while Aleks allows Elinora to hug him – one of the few to whom he grants the privilege.

I find it hard to let go of my friend. *It's been too long, Quinta.*

*Yes it has. You look as exhausted as I know you feel. I'm sorry we're late, I just couldn't pass by Rockwood knowing that Amarilla, Justin and the Kindred are there, and not drop in to see them. Then Mailen insisted we stay and you know…*

I chuckle. *Yes, I know what Mailen's like, but she was right to insist you stay there for a couple of days. You've worked like a maniac since we left The Gathering, what was it now, nearly a year ago? You deserved a little time to yourself before getting here and immersing yourself back into chaos.*

Quinta smiles at all of those who offer their hands for her to shake and Spider to sniff. *I've had a lovely time travelling here and I'm more than ready to get stuck in. How does the saying go? A change of chaos is as good as a rest from chaos.*

*I don't think that's how the saying goes at all,* Aleks interrupts, *but I like it.* He turns to the crowd and yells, 'Who's offering lodging to Ellie and Res, and who to Quinta and Spider? The horses are tired and their Bond-Partners are eager to start work.'

The excitement of welcoming the new arrivals doubles, as does the level of noise as many voices vie to be heard.

*Does your observation about a change of chaos being restful apply to the level of chaos Aleks can generate?* I ask Quinta and we both laugh.

*Show me where to start.*

I bring to the forefront of my mind half of the people Aleks was on his way to see, and half of those from my list. *He and I'll do the other half if you and Elinora are sure you don't mind taking on those?*

*No problem at all,* Quinta replies while verbally thanking a man who is insisting she and Spider lodge with him and his daughter. *And Fitt? Ahh, okay, you leave her to herself in the evenings so she can rebalance herself ready for the morning. Ellie and I are dying to meet her, especially since having met her parents and friends, but we'll not disturb her.*

*We tend to catch up with each other at breakfast and lunchtime. See you tomorrow.* I hug her again and then hug Elinora before leaving them to go on with their evening while I set about returning to my own.

'Well, that will make life easier,' Aleks says as he falls in beside me. 'It'll be an early night for us for a change, and that means you'll have no excuse for being the last one up in the morning. I swear, without those children tearing around like a herd of donkeys, the day would be half gone before you managed to wake up.'

'Because you would absolutely stay out of my head long enough for that to happen,' I retort with a grin. I stop at the gate of a grey stone cottage that looks very similar to all of the rest in Bigwood, glad to be able to use my sense of who is inside to find it rather than having to remember directions. 'This is me, see you in the morning.'

He stoops to kiss me on my forehead. 'I'll be in your head long before that. Rest easy, Sonn.'

'And you.' I watch him for a few moments as he continues on down the street, calling out greetings to everyone he passes. The days are long and not without challenge, but I'm enjoying each and every one.

TWELVE

Aleks
_____

*I*t hasn't been easy, standing back and leaving Fitt to work through her struggles over the past weeks, especially since her progress has been so up and down. There has been a slow improvement in her confidence to be herself from day to day, but a gradual deterioration during each day as her strength and balance have waned under the continual onslaught of fear and horror at her appearance. Regardless, between her, Quinta, Ellie, Shefali, Sonja and me, we have now, in a haphazard kind of a way, helped most of the villagers to get to where they need to be in terms of Awareness and confidence.

There are still some who will need far longer exposure to a Kindred before their minds will open to Awareness, and it is no coincidence that they are not only those holding the most fear of Fitt and her kind, but those who have resisted the idea of Kindred coming to live among them. It is going to happen – the overwhelming majority of the village have agreed to accept those already on their way from Fitt's family community at Shady Mountain, and Quinta and Ellie will be staying to help them settle in. We all have a sense that it will work out, but none of us are under any illusion that it won't be very strange for all concerned to begin with.

It is almost time to move on. Almost – but we haven't quite finished here yet. Fitt can help to ease the way for everyone, if I can persuade her to.

I splash my way through the slush that still clings to the cobbles of Bigwood even though the big melt began nearly a week ago. Most of those I encounter smile and then, as their minds touch mine and sense my dedication to reaching my destination, raise a hand and continue on their way. The less Aware require my verbal confirmation of, 'I can't stop, sorry, have a good morning.' None of them take offence – to a person, they are happy and excited about the new era into which they have embarked, and grateful to those of us who have helped to introduce it.

When I knock on Shefali's door, it is Sonja who opens it. She leans close to me and whispers conspiratorially, 'Quinta and Elinora will be on their way shortly,' as if it's a secret when in fact their intention to meet us once they have finished breakfast alerted all of us concerned.

I grin and whisper back, 'Great, are you going to let me in?'

She kisses me and stands aside. 'Good luck.'

'Luck doesn't exist,' I say, kicking the slush from my boots and stepping inside. 'Charm, however, does.'

Sonja laughs. 'Then good charm.' Before I can say the words she knows I'm going to, she adds, 'Yes, I know that isn't an actual saying and it doesn't make proper sense, but you know what I mean. Go for it, Aleks. If anyone can give her the strength to do this, you can.'

Shefali appears at the end of the hallway wearing oven gloves. 'I've been keeping your breakfast hot for you, Aleks, but it's on the table now.'

I hastily shed my coat and boots, and follow Sonja to the kitchen where we find Shefali now sitting on a thick woven rug of every colour, drinking tea with Fitt. Fitt is careful not to spill any tea from the bowl she is cradling in her hands as she turns to me and says, 'Good morning, my friend. I know you're here to talk to me about something important, though I know not what it is you wish to say since you're all now adept at hiding things from me.' Her eyes flicker to Shefali and we all grin as we sense her grudging admiration for her student.

'As it happens, Shefali doesn't know,' I say, winking at the slight woman with the intense stare, 'and it makes us all happy that you don't know that.'

I am rewarded with smiles from both Fitt and her host. I pick up the tray that is waiting for me on the table, and sit on the floor with my breakfast while Sonja pours herself a cup of tea. I tuck into my bacon and eggs, the smell of them making my stomach rumble loudly, yet not potent enough to block out my sense of Fitt's eyes upon me, or her discomfort.

'Bear with me a moment,' I say with my mouth full, closing it quickly at Shefali's look of disgust. I quickly chew and swallow my food. 'Sorry, I've been up for over an hour and I'm starving. I wanted to check in on Keel and Nita as soon as they were awake because I didn't feel they were where they should have been when I left them last night. The good news is that they are now.'

'I'm sure they were thrilled to find you on their doorstep before they'd even had a chance to get dressed,' Shefali says, her uncharacteristic giggle an attempt to relieve the guilt she senses from Fitt at Keel and Nita having needed extra help as a result of being last to see Fitt yesterday. She may have only had visits from the last few to find the courage to see her, but their reactions to her appearance still accumulated and took their toll.

I wait for the few moments it takes Fitt to move past her

anguish, as she has become so adept at doing, then dive straight in, telling her, 'Your friends from Shady Mountain are on their way here, you know that. Knowlesson and Burtonlee, Lewismar and Hartfill will be here in about a month.'

I sense the warmth in Fitt's heart as her attention turns to those I have mentioned by name for that very reason, and then its ache as I add, 'They walk tall. They use their fangs and talons to hunt. They're used to meeting the eyes of those they live amongst.'

Fitt's green, slitted eyes bore into mine as she begins to see the problem. I have to drive it home. It's why I'm here with her. I chew another mouthful of food slowly before swallowing it, to give her a moment to prepare for that which she now suspects is coming.

'They are two young couples who've left their community and way of life to come here and continue what you've started. They have the chance to live a new kind of life for themselves, hopefully an easier one. Part of our job here is to pave the way for their arrival and with that in mind, it'll help if the villagers are prepared for what they'll see when your friends arrive.' I hold Fitt's stare as I repeat my description of them. 'They'll be walking tall, their fangs and talons will be visible, and they'll no doubt be smiling nervously as they meet the eyes of everyone who'll gather to meet them – everyone who will have been knocked off balance at the sight of them "snarling" and generally behaving so differently from the only Kindred they've met before.'

Fitt flinches and reflexively casts her eyes downward. She places her bowl on the rug in front of her, curls her fingers inward and hunches her shoulders slightly. But then Flame's warmth nudges at her. She welcomes it and it spreads rapidly within her. I'm fascinated to watch Fitt lose and then regain her centre so visibly as she sits back up straight, flexes her fingers and meets my eyes once again.

Her voice is raspier than normal as she says, 'You think I should leave this cottage and ride around the whole village without hiding anything of myself.'

My reply is gentle but firm. 'Your friends – our friends – will be on foot. They won't have horses to ease the way for them.'

'We'll walk with you, Fitt,' Sonja says. 'Me, Aleks, Quinta and Elinora, we'll all come with you.'

Shefali adds, 'And when I know your friends' arrival here is imminent, I'll go and meet them so they won't walk into the village alone.' She reaches forward and puts her hands on Fitt's knees. When Fitt meets her fierce gaze, she says, 'I see you, Fitt. I see who you are inside because you've allowed me to. I alone of all the people in Bigwood know the full extent of your beauty.' She tightens her hold on Fitt's knees and shakes them. 'Show everyone else. Let them see you as I do, know you as I do, then when your friends get here, they'll be welcomed with open arms.'

Fitt shudders and makes herself smaller again. I find the thread that binds the two of us and pull it – not gently, as I've done before, but firmly. She can take it, I can feel it.

Fitt shudders again and I pull even more resolutely on the thread in response. Sonja moves to stand behind Fitt, barely having to bend down to put her face next to Fitt's hairy one as she hugs her. I pull harder still on the thread, refusing to let Fitt shy away from the energy we share – the energy that can give us the strength to cope with anything.

Fitt sits up tall and meets my eyes again. 'I will do it,' she whispers. 'Thanks, Aleks.'

I grin at her. 'Don't mention it.'

There is a knock on the front door. I jump to my feet and put my tray on the table. 'I'll get it.'

'You'll get indigestion too, leaping around like that on a full stomach,' Shefali observes, bringing the hint of a smile to Fitt's face.

'Don't worry, his stomach's well used to it.' Sonja's words follow me down the hall.

I open the door to find Quinta and Ellie smiling at me from the doorstep. Ellie throws her arms around me, telling me, 'I'm so glad you let me hug you now because I'd have had to do it regardless.' She grabs hold of my arms and holds me back from her as if it was I who hugged her. 'I hardly recognise you from the man you were when you first arrived at The Gathering. Honestly, Aleks, I'm so proud of you.' She looks past me and smiles. 'Morning, Fitt. It's a good one for a stroll.'

'It absolutely is,' Quinta says as Shefali and Sonja join Fitt in the hallway behind me. 'The sky's blue, the air's crisp but with a hint of warmth from the sun, and we passed clumps of snowbells in several of the gardens on our way here. Spring is coming!'

'You just have to ignore the slush splashing up your legs and freezing there.' I grin at the sighs and rolled eyes I receive in response to my observation, and say with a bow and flourish of my hand, 'You're welcome, it's what I do.'

Fitt shakes her head and chuckles. I wink at her, Aware that the thread between us has begun to pulse with anticipation. 'Come on, let's do this, slush and all.'

Sonja grins. 'Just as soon as you stop blocking the doorway, Aleks.'

I hold up a hand. 'Already moving.'

# THIRTEEN

# Fitt

*I* have never felt so exposed. So vulnerable. Without Flame at my side, I feel as though my body has ceased to exist and it is my naked soul, its weakness visible for all to see, that follows Aleks down the path. All I have to do is be totally, completely, unashamedly myself, yet the thought terrifies me.

Aleks increases his pull on me so that I am towed along behind him with as much force as if he were pulling me physically. He refuses to let me forget that which I taught him and of which he is here to remind me in return. He is successful. I see the situation as it really is, and let go of everything it is not.

I walk tall. I am She Who Is Flame and I am proud to be who I am. At the thought, I burn with warmth and resolve. The cold that is ferocious in its attempts to bite me can't even get close. I sense Flame standing in the opening to her field shelter, content to monitor my challenge from afar yet intent on nothing else.

My fellow Horse-Bonded offer me nothing more than their company as they spread out in a line with me at its centre, and begin to walk the cobbles of Bigwood's main street. They don't offer their light to me as I walk in their midst, because they know I don't need it. Aleks monitors the thread that binds us but no longer pulls at it. It is down to me now.

Three adult females hurrying in our direction stop in their tracks. They know who I am – or thought they did. None of them have seen me standing tall, only slinking around unobtrusively or sitting on a bale of hay or my horse. None of them have met my gaze long enough to remember it, only having been afforded a glance of sufficient duration for them to receive my broadcast of myself. None of them have seen me smile as I am now, for I spared them having to watch my fangs twist my lips into a snarl. None of them know my mind in its entirety, only the part that begged them to accept me as I helped them to Awareness.

All three females take a step backward, then another as shock and fear at the sight of the real me block them from everything that would have told them their concerns are groundless. I falter, only very slightly, but enough that I can't seem to prevent myself slowing to a stop and casting my eyes downward.

My friends stop beside me and Aleks says, 'Morning all, don't let us divert you.'

His voice rings with the voice of his soul, which calls loudly to mine. I lift my eyes and meet those of the women before me, all of which are wide and frozen in horror. I see behind them the three beautiful souls who agreed to provoke my personality in exchange for me provoking theirs. I recognise the lesson they are highlighting for me and feel a surge of determination to fulfil my side of our agreement, which is only fuelled by the warmth and approval of my horse. My discomfort of only moments before disintegrates to nothing, as if it never was.

I smile again. 'Good morning, Doris, Sunil and Rooth.' I send a blast of gratitude to each of them as I say their names. 'Apologies, we're taking up most of the street, you can barely squeeze by.' I stand aside, as do Aleks and Quinta, and motion for the females to pass us. One of them gulps at the sight of my talons and I almost curl them away, but stop myself. All three look at nothing else as they pass, but I sense their fear subsiding.

'Well, that went well,' Aleks says breezily, and the rest of my friends nod encouragingly as a couple of younglings kicking slush at one another almost run into us. They slide to a stop, grabbing hold of one another in order to stay on their feet.

Sonja and Elinora reach out to steady them further, but they don't see either of my friends. Their eyes slowly work their way from my taloned feet up to my face, which I ensure is smiling.

'You're a little late for school, aren't you, not to mention a little wet?' I ask them.

They both nod, their eyes never leaving mine. My heart swells as I sense them reaching for me in their Awareness, curiosity pushing them past their fear. They find me.

*You're different from before,* one of them informs me.

*I thought you were even more scary different but you're nice different,* the other says. *You should smile more, it makes your eyes look less weird.*

I laugh. *I'll bear that in mind. Get to school with you now, and when you get there, show your teacher in your mind who it was that held you up, that way you won't get in trouble.*

They both grin delightedly and tell me, *Thanks, Fitt.* They link hands and run on their way.

'Yeah, thanks, Fitt,' Aleks says, 'for getting us in trouble when they were already running late.' He grins at me and indicates for us to continue on our way with a sidelong tilt of his head.

As I take my place at his side again, a young couple leap to one side of us in alarm. I see the young adult male who would protect his mate by moving to stand in front of her, but I also see the souls who are next in line to reinforce my learning. There is no reason for fear or offence, for hurt or insecurity, and I would help them to see that in return.

'It's good to see you both again,' I say, standing tall and looking straight at them. My warmth carries my broadcast of myself past the fear that has severed them from their Awareness, and they relax. 'That's better, you just need to centre yourselves now, as Elinora has taught you.' *You're almost there, well done.*

They both stare at me as if seeing me for the first time. *Fitt?* the female ventures.

I smile at her. *Connie.* She doesn't flinch but instead smiles back.

*I'm sorry we, I mean I...* the male begins but I don't let him finish.

*There's no need, Halum. As I said, it's good to see you. You've been working hard with Elinora since I saw you last, and your control over your mind is admirable.*

*Thank you. And for everything you've done for us all.*

*Thank you for everything you've all done for me in return.*

I feel their confusion, their minds probing mine for an explanation and easily finding it for I hold it right at the forefront where they can't miss it. Their eyes light up as they sense the thread linking both of them to me, faint as it is now that our agreement has been fulfilled. Excited, they search for and find the thick thread that thrums with possibility as it holds the two of them together.

*Look for that whenever life feels difficult and then you will feel differently,* I tell them. *Connie, Halum, enjoy your day.*

I walk away from them, my friends at my side. 'Way to go, Fitt,' Elinora says under her breath. Sonja squeezes one of my arms and Quinta the other. Aleks holds his hand over Quinta's head, palm facing me, and makes a big show of wincing when I hit it with my palm as he intended. We all walk on.

It is almost lunchtime by the time we make it even halfway along the street as a result of having stopped to talk to all of those who crossed our path. I am weary as a result of concentrating so hard on seeing the truth of every interaction in order to remain true to myself, but delighted that without exception, I was able to help everyone past their fear of me. A large proportion of the villagers of Bigwood are now much better prepared for the arrival of the four Kindred currently heading in their direction.

*The energy of forgiveness has become strong enough within you that you no longer need dwell within the lesson that has ensured such,* Flame informs me. *It will serve you to leave it behind when the opportunity arises.*

I frown but quickly wipe the expression from my face in case I scare an elderly female hobbling towards me. Then I frown again as I realise my mistake; I am me, and all of those around me need me to be such. And I am confused. I have a sense of what Flame meant, but I can't seem to fit her advice into actions I can take. I am spared from having to think on it further as the opportunity to which she eluded quickly becomes obvious.

Shouting erupts further down the street, drawing my eyes and Awareness to its source. Smoke reaches my nose as I begin to lope behind my friends. I forgive the screaming that erupts as those poking their heads out of windows and doors catch sight of me, and focus on reaching the cottage that is on fire. Its front door stands wide open, revealing an inferno raging inside.

'My mother's upstairs,' wails a stout, middle-aged female cradling a burnt hand. 'I tried to get inside and when I opened the front door, the fire just kind of exploded.'

'We'll have to get Enalda out of the window, I'll fetch my ladder,' a mature male says.

'She'll never get down it,' the female wails. 'Her stomach bug took all her strength, that's why she's in bed. I don't know what can have happened, unless a spark somehow cleared the fireguard in the kitchen and caught the rug.' She puts her hands on her head. 'It's my fault, I built the fire up so it wouldn't go out before I got back. Her house is rammed full of cabinets with all her books, they even line the stairs so they'll take the fire straight to her.' She screams as a downstairs window smashes, spraying glass outward onto the cobbled front garden. Flames burst out of the hole as if desperate for oxygen, and begin to lick up the side of the house.

'So then, we need a water chain,' the male says. 'Everyone, fetch buckets and make a chain from my house to here.'

'We can all earth-sing,' Quinta says urgently. 'We need to lift soil from the fields and hurl it in there to quell the flames. Everyone ready?'

'No,' I reply, an idea forming in my mind that takes my breath away even as it slots into place with Flame's counsel of just minutes ago. 'We won't get it here in time, Enalda's already breathing in smoke. She needs to get out of there now. I can get her out.'

Elinora grabs my arm. 'Fitt, no!'

'Heal her from here,' I say, 'like Amarilla did for Flame. Keep healing the damage the smoke is doing to her airways and I'll try to get her out before the oxygen runs out up there.'

'But you could die,' Elinora replies.

I could. My airways are less efficient at passing oxygen to my blood as a result of the skin thickening with which I constantly battle, and that's only one of the risks I face. I could leave this lifetime prematurely, without having the chance to do everything Flame and I are determined to do. But it isn't that which scares me the most; in doing what only I can do, I will be making it as difficult as possible for the villagers of Bigwood to truly accept me. And that's exactly why I should do it.

'Fitt won't die,' Aleks says. 'Ellie, you and Quinta heal Enalda, and Sonn and I will heal Fitt.'

Sonja nods. 'We're right behind you, Fitt.'

I don't hesitate. I squat slightly and then spring over the picket fence that separates the cobbled garden from the street. I bound past the tubs of bulbs whose shoots are just beginning to peek above the soil, barely registering them as my eyes scan the wall in front of me. I feel as well as see where to aim my talons so as to gain the best hold, and leap at the grey stone wall as if it's one of the thousands of trees I have climbed.

I am Kindred, with all of the strength and abilities of my ancestors. I am She Who Is Flame, with all of the warmth and determination of my horse. I am Fitt. I am Me. I embrace my full power and effortlessly scale the wall to the upstairs window behind which I am Aware Enalda now lies unconscious and on the verge of suffocation, even as my friends heal her airways.

'WOEFUL!' A scream of terror follows the word shouted by one of those still too scared to visit me. The time when it would have pierced my heart seems far away; it doesn't even touch me now.

Ignoring the flames reaching up the wall from the downstairs window to just below my feet, I force my talons between the rocks above the bedroom window and punch the whole window, including its frame, inward. I swing my body through the gaping hole left in its place, and wince as I land on the smashed glass within. Had I stopped to pick the shards out of my toughened skin there and then, the wounds would have barely inconvenienced me, but my leap and subsequent landing beside the bed drive them deep into my feet, causing me to bellow with pain.

'FITT!' Sonja shouts in frustration, knowing she can't heal my wounds while they contain glass.

*Focus on what we can heal,* Aleks tells her as I begin to cough.

I shred the bed covers as I scrape them from the white-haired female lying beneath, then close my fingers as I lift her so as not to do the same to her skin. I hold her to my chest with one arm and use the other to swing back out of the hole in the wall. I twist in the air outside, relieved beyond measure when it replaces the smoke in my lungs, then plunge the talons of my feet between the rocks in the wall.

I climb sideways as much as down in order to avoid the flames roaring out of the downstairs window. I move slowly, carefully, so as to not injure Enalda, whose breathing is easing all the time as Elinora and Quinta continue their work. The elderly female cradled to my chest opens her eyes and gasps, then screams and begins to struggle feebly. My heart goes out to hers, soothing her fear, strengthening her lifeforce and giving her confidence that she is safe in my care. She calms.

I move down the wall even more carefully, my feet balls of agony and dripping blood that begins to sizzle on the grey rocks below, heated as they are by flames from inside. When I can't climb down any further without burning both myself and Enalda, there is only one option left available to me. I take it. I push myself back from the wall with as much force as I can muster and allow myself to fall feet first, holding my charge firmly to my chest with both arms now, determined not to let go of her.

I brace myself for the pain that is unavoidable and, as it turns out, completely untempered by my preparation for it. I land on my ruined feet, driving the glass shards in even further while the muscles in my thighs operate in concert with those that surround my knees and ankles to take the shock out of the landing for Enalda. Pain takes my breath away but I will myself to remain standing until the human in my arms is safe.

# FOURTEEN

## Sonja

For a moment, nobody moves; all of us are stunned at the sight of Fitt blazing with who she is even as blood pools rapidly at her feet. Flames of love, strength and determination burst from her in all directions, far brighter than those of the fire behind her. The frail old lady in her arms clings to her, feeling safer than ever before in her life and loathe to let go.

The sound of hooves clattering on the cobblestones breaks the spell holding us all in place, and everyone moves at once. Enalda's daughter runs to Fitt and tries to lead her further from the flames that are now being attacked with water from buckets arriving along a hastily formed chain of villagers. Fitt can't move for fear she will faint at the agony in her injured feet, so instead gently lowers Enalda to her own feet so that her daughter and Quinta can help her away. Quinta heals the few minor burns Enalda has sustained, and the last of the damage done to her airways, as they go.

Aleks, Elinora and I run to Fitt, holding our hands up to keep the heat from scorching our faces. Her knees buckle as her blood, her life force, continues to be pumped from the severed arteries in her feet and ankles.

'We can't heal them,' Elinora cries, 'not until we've got the glass out.' She gestures to the nearest water bearer. 'Bring that bucket over here and throw the water on the ground to cool it.' She grabs hold of Fitt and leans into her along with Aleks and me.

.'Hang on,' Aleks tells Fitt, 'when the cobbles are wet, you can sit down.'

I turn to those not involved in the attempt to control the fire, and yell, 'Get some tweezers, big ones, QUICKLY!'

Before anyone has a chance to move, Flame bursts out of the smoke billowing down the street, jumps the fence and lands on the cobbles beside us. She ignores the furore that surrounds us and nuzzles Fitt's shoulder. I sense her intention and realise that she is right. She is Fitt's best hope of staying alive.

No one else in Fitt's condition would find the strength to vault onto a horse, but then no one else is Fitt. The second she is astride her horse, Flame jumps the fence again and, in no doubt that their strength will keep Fitt in place on her back, gallops to the village Herbalist's cottage, leaving a bloody trail in her wake.

Everyone rushing to help with the fire is forced to leap to the side of the street so as to not be mown down by the powerhouse that is They Who Are Flame. To a person, they are affected by the energy being flung out in all directions by the Kindred and her Bond-Partner. They stand and stare after them, not in fear but with a concern for Fitt that only increases in those Aware enough to gather what has happened.

'You two go and help the Herbalist,' I say to Aleks and Elinora. 'I have a faint sense of a snowstorm I can divert this way to put the fire out before it reaches the thatching and spreads to the cottages either side.'

They both nod and begin to follow Fitt's bloody trail at a run.

My eyes follow it back to the pools of blood where she landed from the cottage wall, which still seem to blaze ferociously with her strength and determination. I funnel both into my singing.

I don't need to sing out loud but when it comes to the Skill in which I was trained, I prefer to – I love to. I was a strong Weather-Singer before, but now I'm unstoppable. The wind whips up, hurling clouds ahead of it to darken the sky, and by the time some of those nearby sense what I'm doing and come to stand with me in order to join their voices with mine, snow has begun to fall. Before long, there are nine of us singing together, and snow is falling so heavily that the cottage before us almost disappears from view. The flames that were whipped up to even greater ferocity by the wind now shrivel as it blows the cold, wet onslaught through the gaps where the door and windows used to be.

One of those standing with me bends his head to mine so that I can hear him. 'Thanks for drawing it this way until the rest of us could sense it. I think we can all get out of the weather for now. We'll come back and sort out the mess when it's passed.'

I lift a hand in acknowledgement and turn wearily for the Herbalist's cottage. I haven't met her but like Flame before me, I follow my sense of the one to whom the villagers turn when they have need of the energy of herbs, and walk into the wind and snow. I smile to myself as I remember the last time I influenced a weather pattern of this strength; I caused something of a monsoon out on the plains that irritated Aleks no end, and he's never let me hear the last of it. I look forward to hearing his views on this one.

I take a turning off the main street and then turn twice more, into ever narrower streets, before I see as well as sense that I am close to my destination; at least twenty people are huddled before the gate of the Herbalist's cottage with Flame in their midst. Someone has draped a couple of blankets and what appear to be four or five waxed cloaks over the mare's back and neck, and those on the windward side of her all face her, their backs deflecting the weather from her as best they can. Flame stands with her muzzle almost on the ground, giving the appearance of being asleep when in fact she is busy supporting her Bond-Partner.

I sense Aleks and Elinora healing the blood vessels in Fitt's feet as quickly as they can, but they are frustrated by having to wait for the Herbalist to pull shards of glass out of their way first. Fitt has lost a lot of blood and also now her consciousness as a result, but I know her and am completely confident she will pull through.

I make my way through the crowd to Flame and put my hand under the blanket on her neck. She is dry and warm. I turn to the woman closest to me. 'Thank you for taking care of her.'

The woman shrugs, dislodging the snow that was resting on her shoulders. 'It's the least we can do. Hay and buckets of water are on their way. I just wish we could do more for Fitt, but we'll only get in the way in there. They have all the skill and strength they need.' Her words are heartfelt; she cares for Fitt. She met her when she sought her help to reach Awareness, but having witnessed her blazing her way through the village astride Flame, she's now drawn to her without knowing why, and desperate for her to survive.

'Looking after her horse is the best thing you can do for her,' I say. 'You're Aware of what Flame is doing?'

She nods enthusiastically. 'It's like she's sending herself through the wall and surrounding Fitt, holding her together.'

'Yep, she's making her energy available to Fitt as she heals, and to the Healers. She won't leave here until Fitt's stable, so we'll need to carry on shielding her and looking after her as you all have been. I think we need to take it in turns though, it's too rough to be out here for long.'

Another woman speaks up. 'We'll be out here for as long as it takes. You should go inside though. We're Aware of what you've done – Enalda's alive, the fire's out and all of our cottages are safe because of you and Fitt. Now Fitt's injured and you're exhausted. Get yourself indoors to rest, and leave Flame to us.' She puts a hand to my back and gives me a gentle push for emphasis.

I haven't got the strength to argue. 'Thank you.'

I rub Flame's forehead but as expected, she doesn't acknowledge me. Her eyes are almost closed, snowflakes resting undisturbed upon her eyelashes, and her breathing is deep and even. I leave her and make my way up the front path to the cottage. I don't knock for I don't want to disturb those inside. I remove my boots and leave them next to those of Aleks and Elinora just inside the door, then follow the trail of blood along the hallway, wincing at the agony that I know each and every step will have caused my friend.

When I enter the healing room, Fitt is lying on her back on the floor, the Herbalist crouching over her feet. Elinora and Aleks sit cross-legged behind the Herbalist, following her progress within their Awareness. Aleks looks up and winks at me, then points to an armchair with a blanket draped over one arm. *Well done, Sonn. Rest up now, we've got this.*

We are ready to leave Bigwood just two days later. I would have needed at least double that to recover from the injuries Fitt sustained and the subsequent level of healing she required, but as has happened before, her makeup and determination combined to allow her to bounce back in an astonishingly short amount of time.

I stand in the street with Bright, Aleks and Nexus, returning hugs where they are offered and accepting verbal thanks for our visit and our help. I don't need to be Aware to know when Fitt and Flame are approaching – the attention of all of those around me shifts visibly towards the path between Shefali's and Tosca's cottages. Where before the villagers were intimidated by Fitt's differences, now they don't even see them. My friend walks beside her horse, radiating her beauty as obviously as does Flame. She is mesmerising and the villagers flock to her, blocking the path.

*Like moths to a flame,* Aleks observes, very obviously looking around us both to emphasise the fact that we and our horses are now standing alone.

I chuckle. *You've been sitting on that one for a day or two.*

*I have. Now I just want to sit on Nexus and get going.*

'I hope you were planning to say goodbye to us first?' Elinora taps Aleks on the shoulder and hugs him when he turns around.

'We'll miss the six of you,' Quinta says, hugging me.

'The Kindred are only a few days' travel away now,' Aleks replies. 'You won't have time to miss us once they get here. There'll be so much to do, helping them settle in and prepare for more of their community to follow, not to mention helping the last few still holding out against the idea of them being here, to cope with it all.'

'It's exciting, isn't it,' I say. 'And I can't wait to see what happens at the next village on our list.' I nod my head back to where Fitt and Flame are slowly making their way through their admirers.

'I foresee having a problem keeping my attention on what's happening here when I'll be wanting to follow what you're all up to,' Quinta says. She turns to Aleks who is now astride Nexus. 'Are you not going to wait for Fitt?'

He grins. 'We could be waiting all day. She and Flame can catch us up. Coming, Sonn?'

I hug Elinora and then mount Bright, sensing his rapidly increasing eagerness to stretch his legs now that the opportunity has become imminent.

'Bye, everyone,' I call out with a wave as Bright and Nexus fall into step beside one another in the slush.

'Fare you well,' Quinta calls in return, she and Elinora alone in noticing our departure as they stand arm in arm, waving.

'Like moths to a flame,' Aleks repeats with a chuckle as we leave the cobbles behind at a canter.

# Epilogue

*S*moke rises in the distance, beckoning us onward to the village for which we have been heading for the past four days. A flutter of anticipation arises in my belly and spreads to Sonja's, then Fitt's.

Unbidden, our horses move up to a canter, creating a cloud of pollen as the tall meadow grasses part to allow their passage. The sun has been beating down on us for hours and all six of us are hot, sweaty and thirsty, but it isn't the promise of shade and water that now draws us to Sandyfields at speed. After nearly six months of travelling from village to village, we know what will unfold and we are keen to meet it.

As always when Horse-Bonded visit the villages, our approach is noticed well before we are within hailing distance, and by the time we reach the first cottage of stone, a crowd awaits us. As has been the case since Sonja and I began visiting villages in Fitt's company, our arrival has been heralded and it is not a crowd of excited villagers that awaits us but one whose emotions range from curiosity to terror. But as has become usual at all of the villages we have visited since Bigwood, those emotions are rapidly replaced by warmth and excitement.

Nexus and Bright canter to either side of Flame, all three moving as one with the result that all six of us move as one. By the time we reach the crowd, its members are silent. Sonja and I have grown used to taking it in turns to introduce our group, and this time it is Sonja's turn.

She lifts a hand so that all eyes turn to her. 'Villagers of Sandyfields, I am Sonja and this is my Bond-Partner, Bright. That's Aleks with Nexus, and between us are Fitt and Flame.'

All eyes rest upon the two who burn with the truth of who they are, and all souls reach for them in response.

'Everything the Heralds have told you is true,' Sonja says. 'Fitt of the Horse-Bonded and the Kindred is here to help you know yourselves for who you really are. You already have a sense of what that means; you all feel who she is and what she's about. Once she has helped you to Awareness, more Kindred are willing to come here to live amongst you, to help you become accustomed to using it.'

The villagers are still listening to her but they barely take in her words. Five of them are already Aware, the first of whom Fitt guides to me.

*Aleks?*

*Welcome to Awareness, Dana. Wilf, hello, oh and here's Piet.*

By the time I have dismounted, all of the people in front of us are Aware of exactly how hot and thirsty the six of us are.

As is usual, Sonja and I are offered lodgings once Fitt and Flame's has been agreed, and then the bombardment of newly Aware minds on ours continues as our friend works her magic on newcomers to the crowd.

It isn't really magic though. I know exactly what it is.

When I first met Fitt, she stunned me by forgiving the people, the energy, of The Old. When we were in Bigwood, she forgave over and over those who were scared of her and she forgave herself even more frequently, until she was instantly able to see the souls of those before her and recognise the agreement they had made with her own. She is now so strong in the energy of forgiveness that she has the strength to wholly be her warm, compassionate, determined self. She no longer merely broadcasts who she is, she blazes with it and She Who Is Flame is very powerful.

From forgiveness has come strength.

Sonja senses my realisation. *That's what Bright told me would happen, back when we left Rockwood in that blizzard. He put it a bit more eloquently though.*

*That's a little rude, though I don't doubt it's true. How did he put it?* My question draws the answer to the forefront of her mind.

*From a spark comes a flame.*

I nod in appreciation. *Nice.*

# Other Books by Lynn Mann

The Horses Know Trilogy
The Horses Know
The Horses Rejoice
The Horses Return

Sequels to The Horses Know Trilogy
Horses Forever
The Forgotten Horses
The Way Of The Horse

Prequels to The Horses Know Trilogy
In Search Of Peace (Adam's story)
The Strength Of Oak (Rowena's story)
A Reason To Be Noble (Quinta's story)

Tales Of The Horse-Bonded (Short Story Collection)

A regularly updated book list can be found at
www.lynnmann.co.uk/booklist
Use the QR code below for easy access:

Did you enjoy From A Spark Comes A Flame?
I'd be extremely grateful if you could spare a few minutes
to leave a review where you purchased your copy.
Reviews really do help my books to reach a wider audience,
which means that I can keep on writing!
Thank you very much.

I love to hear from you!
Get in touch and receive news of future releases at the following:

www.lynnmann.co.uk

www.facebook.com/lynnmann.author

# Acknowledgments

I have long since given up trying to have any control over which story I'll write next from the world of the Horse-Bonded; it's always a case of having various characters simmering away at the back of my mind, and listening to the one who shouts loudest at any given time. Having often wondered what Fitt, Flame and their friends got up to after the end of The Horses Rejoice, I still wrote eight books before getting around to discovering/creating their story, and it's a relief to finally have done so!

I would like to thank you, my readers, for following me on my writing journey as I've darted back and forth within timelines and between worlds. Doing so has kept my mind fresh and my writing time exciting and immensely enjoyable.

Huge thanks as always to my editorial team – Fern Sherry, Leonard Palmer, Caroline Macintosh and Cindy Nye – whose help and support goes far beyond the invaluable work they do on my manuscripts.

I'm immensely grateful to Jon Morris of MoPhoto for allowing his shot of our very beautiful mare, Eden, to be used on the cover of the book, and to Amanda Horan for making such amazing use of it in her cover design.

Eden was the inspiration for Flame's character as well as being our cover model. She really is the warmest, most affectionate mare who has the ability to hold away from herself everything that isn't her. As a result, being in her company is always an immensely grounding, soul-soothing experience. My husband and I adopted Eden into the Mann Clan partly because she was lame and needed help, and partly because it was impossible not to feel her reaching out to us. We're so glad we did!

Manufactured by Amazon.ca
Bolton, ON

34442975R00077